D0910126

COLUMBIA STUDIES IN ECONOMICS

4

BANKERS' DIPLOMACY

MONETARY STABILIZATION IN THE TWENTIES

RICHARD HEMMIG MEYER

BANKERS'
DIPLOMACY

MONETARY STABILIZATION
IN THE TWENTIES

1970
COLUMBIA UNIVERSITY PRESS
New York and London

Copyright © 1968, 1970 Columbia University Press
SBN: 231-03325-7
Library of Congress Catalog Card Number: 79-111120
Printed in the United States of America

To Luciane

WHOSE UNDERSTANDING, ENCOURAGEMENT,

AND SACRIFICE

MADE THIS WORK POSSIBLE

PREFACE

Since this study was sponsored by the Department of Economics, Columbia University, and was provided financial support through an economics fellowship granted by the Ford Foundation, some preliminary comment about its orientation might be appropriate. In particular, it may be advisable to warn the reader at the outset that the study is as much, and perhaps more, concerned with matters of political science as it is with questions of economics in any narrow sense. The reader who is expecting a theoretical analysis or an empirical testing of hypotheses based upon fundamental economic principles will be gravely disappointed.

This warning, however, is in no way intended as an apology for the orientation that has been adopted. On the contrary, I have deliberately attempted to make this study a work in political economy in the somewhat outmoded, but most comprehensive, meaning of that term. Such a focus of interest requires, in my opinion, no justification. In fact, it is my profound conviction that the dropping out of fashion of the use of the qualification "political" in designating that field of study which has become known simply as economics has unfortunate implications. The elimination of the qualifying term has resulted from, and in turn has encouraged, a concentration on the purely technical aspects of economic problems such as efficient resource allocation and product distribution. This is not meant to imply, of course, that such concentration on technicalities is per se without value or is in some sense misguided. But such concentration on the part of the profession as a whole tends to encourage excessively narrow specialization in the interests of technical rigor. In particular, such specialization tends to result in a situation in which the study of the interaction of political and economic activity falls somewhere between the provinces of the political scientist and the economist where it is inadequately considered by both.

I am convinced that politics and economics are so closely intertwined, especially in the international sphere, that the two must be considered inseparable. To attempt to deal with the economics independently of the politics is to run the risk of missing the most interesting and the most significant causes and consequences of international behavior. In fact, much of the problem discussed in this study arose precisely because of the acceptance of the untenable assumption that international economic activity could somehow be separated from international politics—an assumption not unfamiliar today.

The activities of the central bankers dealt with in this study necessarily involved matters of great concern to their respective foreign offices. The actions taken by the central bankers were frequently certain to be either in support of or disruptive of the foreign policy of their own nations. Yet there seems to have been little consciousness of this fact on the part of the central bankers and, in the case of the United States Department of State at least, on the part of the foreign office. Only in the Rumanian case did the question arise in the United States, and the issue then was more one of domestic political impact than it was of the influence of Federal Reserve international activities on the national foreign policy goals.

This lack of concern on the part of the central bankers and politicians alike was, however, no oversight. There were, in fact, many formal international expressions in the 1920s of the notion that international economic activity could and should be divorced from international politics. One need only cite the recommendations of the 1920 Brussels Conference and the resolutions of the Genoa Conference in 1922. Thus both the central bankers and the politicians were convinced that their fields of activity fell into distinctly separate compartments which should not be concerned with each other. The record of the stabilization negotiations is a graphic demonstration of the unreasonableness of this assumption.

If international politics and international economics are indeed inseparable, the problem becomes one of conducting international economic affairs in a way that will minimize their contribution to international political tensions and that will minimize the distortions in economic activity introduced by political considerations. It is not a question of separating the two, but rather of adopting an institutional framework that comes as close as possible to integrating the two on an international, rather than a national, level. This book is directed to precisely this problem in the belief that history, while not repeating itself, can none the less provide valid guides for policy.

As is the case in any work of this type, there are so many who have contributed in one fashion or another that adequate acknowledgment is virtually impossible. Nevertheless, I should like to express my appreciation to a few organizations and individuals whose contributions have been particularly direct and notable.

The financial assistance provided by a dissertation fellowship from the Ford Foundation was welcome as much for the liberal terms under which it was offered as for its generosity. The Federal Reserve Bank of New York was most unstinting in making available essential material from its files. Mr. Robert G. Link was very helpful in arranging for facilities and assistance for this purpose and in reviewing the final manuscript. Mr. Stephen V. O. Clarke, whose outstanding work on central bank cooperation in the 1920s had not yet been published, was generous in the extreme in sharing his expertise in the field. Much time was saved as a result of the insights he provided. A great deal of time and effort was also spared me by Mrs. Evelyn Knowlton, who was invaluable in sorting out pertinent files from the archival mass and in guiding the research in numerous other useful ways.

My debt to the economics faculty at Columbia University is as boundless as it is diffused over numerous individuals of that faculty. Two of these individuals, Professors Harold Barger and Peter B. Kenen, deserve special mention not only as sponsors of this particular work but as general mentors who have always stood ready to give freely of their valuable time and extensive knowledge. Thanks are due as well to Professors Albert G. Hart and Phillip Cagan for reading the manuscript and providing useful and stimulating comment. In addition, Professor Shepard B. Clough of the Department of History and Professor Richard N. Gardner of the Law Faculty furnished most penetrating comment on the manuscript.

Finally, some expression of gratitude is due my wife, who served at various times and without complaint as devil's advocate, editorial adviser, typist, and lightening rod for a frayed temper.

Great as the contributions of these and others to this work have been, the responsibility for any factual or other errors which may remain in these pages is entirely my own. The conclusions and opinions expressed here are mine alone and not necessarily those of the Ford Foundation, the Federal Reserve Bank of New York, or any other institution or individual who aided me in the study.

December 1, 1969   RICHARD HEMMIG MEYER

CONTENTS

CONTENTS

Chapter I. INTRODUCTION

> . . . when a country is clearly in such an unbalanced position that radical measures are required to restore equilibrium, private banks may properly be deterred by the risks involved in granting it further credit facilities. In such situations, it is only if a comprehensive program is adopted and put into effect that the risk will be reduced; and private institutions are not in a position to negotiate such programs. Experience has shown that the Governments in the various countries are more willing to discuss and work out stabilization programs with officials of the Fund than with representatives of other countries or of private credit institutions. [1]

These words of Mr. Per Jacobsson, former Managing Director of the International Monetary Fund, succinctly summarize the part which the Fund has played in stabilization operations since its founding, and which it is hoped it will continue to play. The Fund has performed a necessary and useful function in assisting nations in financial distress in developing and adhering to comprehensive programs to put their monetary and fiscal houses in order. By so doing, it has contributed to the restoration of the credit standing of those nations and prepared the way for the needed influx of private capital. Whether the governments of these nations always preferred

[1] "Fund Report at ECOSOC," *International Financial News Survey,* April 10, 1959, p. 315.

to deal with the officials of the Fund rather than with representatives of other countries may be open to some question, but in the post-World War II world they had little choice. The availability of drawing rights on the Fund made of it the institution to which a nation in difficulty naturally turned first. Just as naturally, it led to supplementary assistance being provided through the Fund or at least to its being provided in conjunction with International Monetary Fund aid. There are increasing indications, however, that the Fund's position as a focal point for such international transactions is breaking down.[2]

In the world of the 1920s, however, the situation was quite different. The nearest approximation to an institution such as the International Monetary Fund which could undertake to negotiate and supervise such comprehensive programs was the Financial Committee of the League of Nations. The nations in serious financial difficulties at that time showed a somewhat surprising reluctance to turn to that Committee. Prior to 1926, the only such programs developed through the Financial Committee of the League were those for Austria and Hungary—both nations which had been on the losing side in World War I. This, in itself, may have been sufficient for ex-Allied nations to feel some reluctance about turning to the League for

[2] The aid furnished Britain in June 1966 was furnished through the Bank for International Settlements, not through the International Monetary Fund, and two of the eleven nations providing support did so directly rather than by joining the others and channeling their aid through the Bank for International Settlements (*The New York Times*, June 14, 1966, pp. 65, 73). Similarly, the central bank aid to sterling in November 1967 was clearly distinguished from government aid provided through the International Monetary Fund. France chose to participate in the IMF loan (with some delay and reluctance) but refused to join in a central bank credit. It is interesting to note that part of the reason for that refusal is alleged to have been that ". . . the French have been saying that the loan to Britain should be channeled through the I.M.F., thus permitting a measure of international control that would not be possible if the creditors were individual countries" (*The New York Times*, November 20, 1967, pp. 1, 74). The Bonn meetings of November 1968, which attempted to deal with an apparent franc-mark imbalance, were clearly meetings of the Finance Ministers and central bank Governors of the Group of Ten nations called by the Minister of Economics of the Federal Republic of Germany. The Managing Director of the IMF seems to have attended in a capacity similar to that of the Secretary-General of the Organization for Economic Cooperation and Development and the Vice-President of the Commission of the European Communities, i.e., as an interested observer ("Communiqué of Ministerial Meeting of Group of Ten," *International Financial News Survey*, November 29, 1968, p. 397).

assistance. Perhaps more significant, however, was the fact that the League plans provided stringent controls, particularly over the use of the proceeds of the long-term loan and over the revenues forming the principal security for the loan.[3] Such stringent control need not necessarily have been part of a League plan in support of a nation in less desperate condition than Austria and Hungary. It was, however, part of the only two plans which the League had as yet developed and it appears to have been assumed that it would be part of any additional plans prepared by the League. In any event, from the end of 1925 the practice developed of turning, not to the League of Nations, but to one or more of the major national central banks for assistance. The major central bank or banks would then negotiate with the government and the central bank of the stabilizing nation, with the private bankers who were to extend credits or handle long-term loan issues, and with other central banks in order to arrive at a program which was acceptable to all and which had reasonable prospects for success. On the basis of such a program and the assurance of private loan or credit assistance, a consortium of central banks would then be organized to provide credit assistance to the central bank of the stabilizing country.

This study will trace the history of the negotiation of such loans and credits in the years 1926–1928 in the case of four stabilizing nations: Belgium, Italy, Poland, and Rumania. The focus of interest will be on the impact of these negotiations on the relationships among the major central banks (the Federal Reserve Bank of New York, the Bank of England, and the Bank of France). It will be argued that the negotiations themselves were a serious and unnecessary source of division in the relations of the major central banks. The negotiations were, of course, far from being the only source of disruption in those relations, but they contributed much to driving the central banks apart and thus helping to destroy any reasonable basis for international monetary and financial cooperation. It will be shown that there is considerable question as to how essential the loans and credits were in enabling the nations concerned to achieve monetary stabilization. But even if one accepts the idea that early

[3] League of Nations Economic, Financial and Transit Department, *The League of Nations Reconstruction Schemes in the Inter-War Period* (Geneva, 1945).

stabilization was desirable and that the loans and credits were essential for this purpose, the damage inflicted on central bank relations by the negotiations was a very high and, it will be argued, an unnecessary price to pay for the attainment of this goal.

The difficulty seems to have stemmed from ad hoc efforts to achieve some sort of coordinated multilateralism. Since the efforts were ad hoc, each transaction had to be dealt with individually so that conflicting interests necessarily became embroiled in and deepened by each negotiation. A case can be made for the idea that an outright bilateral approach would have been politically preferable to the course actually adopted. This was, however, unnecessary since the Financial Committee of the League provided a natural, if imperfect, institution through which a more permanent form of multilateralism could have been achieved.[4] The use of the Financial Committee as a focal point would have tended to put the political issues on a policy level rather than have them become details in the negotiation of each transaction.

The history of the negotiation of these loans and credits brings out the crucial importance of institutionalizing such international monetary and financial cooperation. The establishment of the Bretton Woods institutions at the close of World War II was precisely an effort in this direction. Based upon the 1926–1928 experience, it will be argued that any move away from such institutionalization, even though sometimes difficult to avoid because of technical considerations, is a dangerous step. Undesirable as they might be, however,

---

[4] The League was quite imperfect for this purpose, not least because of the fact that the United States was not a member and, by the late 1920s, was deep in its policy of isolation from Europe in general and the League in particular. Still, this was no necessary bar to Federal Reserve participation since the government had no legal control over such activities of the Federal Reserve (see fn. 14, p. 12) and the leading personality of the Reserve in the mid-1920s, Benjamin Strong, was not easily dominated by political pressure. In any event, the League was the only institution available at the time. The Bank for International Settlements, a more appropriate institution for the purpose, was not founded until 1931 and then as part of the Young Plan reparations settlement, not as a focal point for general monetary cooperation. Nevertheless, it quickly assumed this role of focal point and, despite the fact that the Federal Reserve was prevented by the United States government from taking up membership, it participated in joint credits organized by the BIS. See, for example, Eleanor Lansing Dulles, *The Bank for International Settlements at Work* (New York, 1932), p. 395.

some limited bilateral moves—such as some forms of foreign aid and technical assistance—may be required for such technical or other reasons. But it must be recognized that such steps tend to weaken the effectiveness of the international organizations; hence, they should be accepted only to the extent that they are absolutely essential. Moves in the direction of ad hoc multilateralism, such as the modern "swap" arrangements and the General Arrangements to Borrow, are perhaps even more dangerous. Involving, as they do, the necessity for separate negotiation of each transaction among the independent institutions, they open the way for a repetition of the pattern of 1926–1928.

The principal concentration of this study will be on the Polish and Rumanian transactions, since it was in these negotiations that the confusion and disagreement arose. But the Belgian example provided the precedent for avoiding the League of Nations and relying on direct central bank cooperation. Both the Belgian and Italian experience provide a base of reference, and certain aspects of both were appealed to as providing the precedent for disputed provisions and procedures of the Polish and Rumanian negotiations.

The negotiations must be viewed in the light of the general framework of ideas concerning postwar monetary reconstruction prevalent at the time.[5] Few of these ideas would be widely accepted without qualification today, but many of the positions adopted during the negotiations are only intelligible when considered in the perspective of the thought of the times. For example, the eagerness with which the central banks moved to assist a proposed stabilization effort is explicable in part by the prevailing conviction that a return by each nation to a fixed gold parity at the earliest possible moment was clearly desirable. This belief resulted, of course, in a country-by-country approach to stabilization with little attention paid to the vital question of the viability of exchange ratios.[6] The question of

[5] This general framework was given formal international expression in the recommendations of the Brussels Conference in 1920 and the resolutions of the Genoa Conference in 1922. See particularly: League of Nations Economic and Finance Section, *Brussels Financial Conference 1920: The Recommendations and their Application.* (Geneva, 1922), Vol. I, and J. Saxon Mills, *The Genoa Conference* (New York, undated).

[6] W. Randolph Burgess, then Economic Advisor of the Federal Reserve Bank of New York, argues that postwar stabilization was not a series of uncoordinated,

the value of the gold parity was viewed as a sovereign national choice and the chief concern of the central bankers was whether stabilization could be maintained at the chosen rate. Only rarely, and never seriously, was the question raised that the currency might be unduly undervalued.

There was never any question but that the basis of the monetary system should be gold, but the idea that widespread use of the gold exchange standard should be encouraged is another matter. It is an interesting question how this idea came to be embodied in the resolutions of the Genoa Conference, but there can be no doubt that the vast majority of the central bankers of the time viewed it with disfavor.[7] More serious was the fact that most nations who adopted it, and most of them had to at the start, looked upon it as a kind of halfway house to a return to a gold specie, or at least a gold bullion, standard.

One reason for the failure to pay serious attention to the question of the viability of exchange ratios was the trust in the gold standard view of the international adjustment process.[8] This was, after all, a pre-*General Theory* world and it was believed that any imbalance

---

unilateral actions because, generally, a stabilization credit was extended to the central bank concerned by other central banks. Before extending such credits, the central bankers first had to be satisfied with a more or less comprehensive stabilization plan that included, among other things, the proposed parity for the currency (W. Randolph Burgess, *The Reserve Banks and the Money Market* [New York and London, 1946], p. 359). As pointed out above, however, the central bankers concerned themselves with the parity problem only from the point of view of the capacity of the stabilizing country to maintain the chosen rate. Even then, as in the case of Italy, they bowed eventually to national sovereignty. In the most significant case, that of France, no central bank credit was involved.

[7] A variety of material in the files of the Federal Reserve Bank of New York, the Benjamin Strong Papers (Federal Reserve Bank of New York), and the George Leslie Harrison Collection (Columbia University) makes clear that at least Strong and Harrison of the Federal Reserve Bank of New York; Moreau, Rist, and Moret of the Bank of France; Schacht of the Reichsbank; Stringher of the Bank of Italy; Franck of the Bank of Belgium; Bachmann of the Swiss National Bank; and Mlynarski of the Bank of Poland were opposed to the gold exchange standard. Although I was unable to ascertain the precise position of the Bank of England on this point, it must be presumed either that they believed in it and pushed it through at Genoa or that the concept had its origins among the political leaders.

[8] As Stephen Clarke expresses it, "The authorities perceived only dimly, if at all, that in a system managed by national central banks the process of international adjustment was likely to be far slower and more difficult than it was supposed to be under the gold standard conception" (Stephen V. O. Clarke, *Central Bank Cooperation: 1924–31* [New York, 1967], p. 43).

would ultimately correct itself by an adjustment of relative price levels and a return to "normalcy." It was, of course, recognized that the transition period might involve temporary strains. The application of deflationary policies was likely to bring on reduced industrial output and unemployment and then to be followed by the danger of gold inflation resulting from a return flow of capital following a restoration of confidence. The adjustment, however, was seen purely as a problem for the stabilizing nation, without serious impact on other nations. In view of the inflationary experience of the immediate postwar period, it is not surprising that the emphasis was clearly on the side of deflation.[9] No one doubted that deflation was necessary; the only concern was that it should not be so severe as to result in serious social unrest. On the other hand, renewed inflation, from whatever source, was to be avoided at all cost.

This deflationary bias was reflected in the area of fiscal policy as well. The achievement of budgetary equilibrium was regarded as a fundamental prerequisite for effective stabilization. The inflation that was at the root of the currency depreciation was, in fact, largely fiscally induced. The credit standing of the nations concerned had deteriorated to a point where long-term borrowing was virtually impossible even at a high price. The counterpart of the fiscal deficits

[9] The deterioration of the internal value of most Continental currencies in the immediate postwar period was, of course, a consequence of the excessive creation of money in an effort to meet the huge costs of reconstruction and relief. Such resort to the printing press also contributed to the deterioration of the external, or exchange, value of these same currencies. But appreciable deterioration of the exchange value of Continental currencies would have taken place in any case. In view of the general shortage of goods and the destruction and disruption of productive capacity, a large part of the resources for reconstruction and relief had to come from abroad in the immediate postwar years. Thus the exchange value of the currency was neccessarily under pressure. A formal devaluation to adjust the exchange value to this essentially temporary situation, however, would have led to an exchange rate that was inappropriate for more normal conditions. A deflationary policy designed to maintain or restore the prewar exchange value, on the other hand, was likely to increase the shortage of domestic goods and delay the reconstruction effort. The effect, then, of such a policy would have been to increase domestic difficulties while, perhaps, aggravating the pressure on the exchange value as it became increasingly necessary to turn to foreign sources for urgent construction requirements. By 1926, however, a large part of the reconstruction had been accomplished and the exchange difficulties of the currencies under consideration here were, indeed, a consequence of inflationary monetary policies. Except in the case of Italy, the nations considered approached external balance more through formal devaluation than through deflation, although calling a halt to the inflationary process was, of course, an essential part of the stabilization schemes.

then became a huge floating debt largely in the form of advances from the central bank, which, of course, represented money creation. In order to halt the vicious cycle, it was considered essential that the government's access to the central bank be carefully controlled. This, in turn, could only be enforced if the fiscal deficits were eliminated. Thus, the assurance that budget equilibrium had been, or would be, attained was demanded before a loan or credit would be considered.

The final element in this general framework of ideas concerning the postwar monetary system is especially relevant for this study. It was generally agreed that monetary policy should be in the hands of central banks that were free from government control and that these banks should cooperate among themselves uninfluenced by political considerations. Such cooperation would permit, it was felt, the lifting of economic problems out of their political setting so that they could be dealt with on the basis of economic considerations alone. But, while there could be general agreement about the broad principle, there was considerable room for disagreement over its application. Lurking in the statement of the principle are several semantic issues which were never resolved and which, indeed, may not be amenable to precise resolution.

How, for example, does one define "central bank cooperation"? It was agreed that the concept meant, in part, that each central bank should contribute, within the limitations of its resources, to credit extensions to other central banks in difficulty, provided only that conditions were such that the credit would serve a useful purpose. Naturally, there was room for disagreement as to whether or not the appropriate conditions existed. But there were also varying views as to how the potential usefulness of the credit would be evaluated— individually by each participating bank, through some sort of consensus, or on the basis of accepting the assurances of the leader of the consortium.

It was also agreed that cooperation should be expected only to the extent that there was no sacrifice of national interest.[10] But what

---

[10] For example, the *Report of the Gold Delegation* states: "Those responsible for monetary policy in each country must take account both of domestic and of international considerations and these may not be easily reconcilable. It is for this reason that we attach particular importance to the development of

constitutes a sacrifice of national interest? There can be no doubt that, to some extent, every nation's interest is bound up with the general welfare; but the two are rarely identical. If one defines the national interest broadly enough, national interest and the general welfare begin to merge. If one defines it narrowly enough, little scope for cooperation remains. With each nation free to draw the line between the two according to its own judgment, it was quite possible for two nations to follow mutually contradictory courses, each sincerely convinced that it was the other which was not cooperating. One of the virtues of an international institution is that it provides an arbiter, however imperfect, in such issues.

Similar semantic issues are raised by the attempt to avoid the influence of political considerations. How, precisely, is the term "political consideration" to be defined? Is its meaning, in the context of the principle of central bank cooperation, to be limited to questions of foreign policy? Or, is it to mean that, in considering whether or not to extend a loan or credit to the government or central bank of a nation, one is to be uninfluenced by the internal political stability or instability in that nation? The question is not as irrelevant or ridiculous as it seems to be. Even if the meaning of the term is restricted to international political questions, is it possible—with the best of intentions—to separate them from the economic problems? Is not the refusal to consider outstanding political controversies in itself the assumption of a political position in favor of the status quo? At the national level, economics and politics are so inextricably bound together that it would seem that any economic act necessarily has a political impact.

---

methods of continuous consultation and co-operative effort to maintain the international equilibrium without sacrificing national interests" (League of Nations, *Report of the Gold Delegation of the Financial Committee* [Geneva, 1932], p. 50).

Chandler quotes a letter of August 24, 1925, from Benjamin Strong to J. H. Case in which Strong wrote:

"Besides that we were strongly of the opinion that nothing in the way of a formal conference between banks of issue would prove to be feasible, as they would always be influenced by the necessity for a central bank to give consideration to local problems, in preference to international problems; and that each central bank should be entirely free to do so; but that, where there was no conflict with domestic interests, they should endeavor to cooperate" (Lester V. Chandler, *Benjamin Strong, Central Banker* [Washington, 1958], p. 338).

It would appear that the best that could have been expected was that the central bankers would make their own independent evaluation of an economic problem, not without consideration of political issues, but free from pressure to adopt the official position of their governments. Here the legal independence of the central bank vis-à-vis the government becomes important, but not necessarily decisive. The character of the bank's chief executive officer is, perhaps, as significant as the bank's legal position. Regardless of his legal status, any central banker occupies a position which is at least semi-official. He is to some extent responsible to his government and he must work closely with the Treasury. A weak banker is easily dominated and a strong one can resist a surprising amount of pressure even though his legal position is precarious.[11]

In the context of this study, it is surprising to find absolutely no evidence of any such pressure, in the sense that pressure on any of the major central bankers caused them to adopt positions contrary to the dictates of their own judgment. This is not to say, however, that their positions, except for some aspects of Benjamin Strong's activities, were in any way inconsistent with the foreign policy of the government. On the contrary, the positions adopted by Montagu Norman and Émile Moreau might have been determined in their respective Foreign Offices. The point is that they seem to have adopted these positions because they believed in that foreign policy, not because they were obliged to support it.

It is obviously beyond the scope of this work to attempt even a

[11] For example, Governor Moreau, whose appointment was revocable almost at will by the Minister of Finance, successfully resisted flagrant pressure to make advances to the French Treasury. On July 26, 1926, Poincaré asked Moreau for an advance against Treasury bills to be discounted by the Bank of France. When Moreau refused, he replied: "l'Opération que je propose a été faite maintes fois en 1923 et en 1924, par votre prédécesseur, M. Robineau, sans aucune difficulté. Si vous n'y consentez pas, je rappellerai M. Robineau. . . ." [The transaction which I propose was performed many times in 1923 and 1924 by your predecessor, M. Robineau, without any difficulty. If you do not consent to it, I shall recall M. Robineau. . . .] The next day, he again reminded Moreau: "Monsieur le Gouverneur, je vous rappelle que vous êtes un fonctionnaire, nommé par le Gouvernement. Je vous retire la parole." [Monsieur Governor, let me remind you that you are a civil servant, appointed by the government. I forbid you to speak.] But Moreau stood his ground, the advances were not made, and Moreau remained as Governor of the Bank of France (Émile Moreau, *Souvenirs d'un gouverneur de la Banque de France* [Paris, 1954], pp. 45–46).

brief review of the international political setting in which these stabilization negotiations took place or of the foreign policy aims of
the various nations concerned. This would be a huge task in itself
and there is already a large literature on the subject.[12] But this political setting, particularly as it affected policy aims in Eastern Europe, played an extremely large and at times crucial role in the negotiations. It must be constantly kept in mind and will, of course, be
touched upon at the appropriate points. In particular, Émile Moreau, like the majority of Frenchmen, sincerely believed that the
only hope for peace for France and for the world lay in rigid
maintenance of the status quo of Versailles. To this end, it was necessary, not only to avoid scrupulously any concessions to Germany,
but to keep Germany encircled by a ring of states loyal to France. In
Eastern Europe this policy would serve the double purpose of seal-
ing off the Bolshevik menace and preventing its spilling over particularly into Germany. If support of this political policy entailed an
attempt to extend French financial influence in Eastern Europe, so
much the better. Such extension was desirable in any case to counter
the extension of sterling influence, which Moreau mistrusted heart-
ily.

On the other hand, Montagu Norman, as a good, conservative
Englishman, believed just as sincerely that a gradual revision of the
more punitive provisions of Versailles was essential if the European
peace was to be maintained. This view led, of course, to a rather
pro-German outlook which was strengthened by the great respect he
felt for Hjalmar Schacht, President of the Reichsbank. While it
would be going too far to imply that the corollary of Norman's German sympathies was an anti-Eastern European attitude, he had no
particular interest in strengthening the nations of that area. Certainly, he had no desire to support the extension of either French
political or financial influence in that area, particularly at a time
when he was all too conscious of the franc challenge to sterling.

12 Some useful works in this connection are: John O. Crane, *The Little Entente* (New York, 1931); Hugh Seton-Watson, *Eastern Europe between the Wars
1918–1941* (Hamden, Conn., 1962); John W. Wheeler-Bennett, *The Wreck of
Reparations* (New York, 1933); Wheeler-Bennett and Hugh Latimer, *Information
on the Reparation Settlement* (London, 1930); Arnold Wolfers, *Britain and
France between Two Wars* (New York, 1940).

Benjamin Strong also seemed to sympathize with the official policy of his government that America should avoid involvement in European controversies. That such an attitude was not quite compatible with his active promotion of central bank cooperation is evident. Nevertheless, he seems to have held both views and reconciled them in his mind by the notion that central bank cooperation only involved the relationships between the Federal Reserve Bank of New York and its foreign correspondents. He was, in fact, scrupulous about avoiding any form of formal contact with representatives of foreign governments and, in principle, would not even consider informal contacts except in conjunction with the head of the appropriate central bank.[13] Although his activities in this area were hardly consistent with a national policy of isolation, the foreign activities of the Federal Reserve Bank of New York were never seriously questioned until the time of the founding of the Bank for International Settlements when the government decided that Federal Reserve subscription to that bank would be incompatible with United States policy in respect of the reparations issue.[14]

While the loan and credit negotiations took place in a political setting which cannot be ignored, however, the ostensible objective of the loan and credit extensions was not to further the political aims of the participating nations. No matter how strongly he may have

[13] Even with respect to the United States government, both Strong and Harrison were extremely careful to avoid any intimation that they were required to secure, or had requested, the approval of the government to enter into any type of foreign business. They always requested and secured the approval of the Federal Reserve Board, however, before consummating a foreign credit. But in this period, this seems to have been in the nature of a courtesy gesture since neither Strong nor Harrison felt that it was legally required of them. In addition, the New York Bank shared participation in the credits with the other Reserve Banks. All the other Reserve Banks invariably elected to participate, but again, one has the impression that their participation was a courtesy gesture, this time to the New York Bank. One has the feeling that they were rather disinterested. On the other hand, one gets the impression that the Board rather disapproved but was unable or unwilling to refuse the requests of the New York Bank. Certainly, the Board was sometimes uneasy about possible political criticism of these transactions.

[14] Mrs. Dulles points out that this action was, in fact, extralegal since the Administration had no legal authority to bind the Federal Reserve in this matter (see fn. 4, p. 4) (E. L. Dulles, *The Bank for International Settlements at Work*, p. 83). This is another indication of the fact that the legal position of the central bank is not, in itself, enough to determine the extent of its independence with respect to the government.

been influenced by such considerations, no central banker would admit that such factors entered into his calculations. The sole admitted purpose of the credit and loan was to assist another nation to achieve a stable currency, a worthy goal in itself. For this purpose, the loan and the credit, while complementary, served somewhat different functions.

The loans were extended by private bankers to the government of the stabilizing nation and, from a stabilization point of view, were intended to serve one or more major purposes. In some cases, part of the loan was used for developmental purposes (itself a source of controversy) but, in principle, such use was unrelated to the loan as an instrument of stabilization. In modern times, such loans are viewed primarily as a prerequisite for achieving budgetary balance and as a means of providing time in which the nation can make necessary balance of payments adjustments without undue internal strain. The stabilization loans of the 1920s served these purposes, of course, although in the cases considered by this study, this function was not stressed. The principal purpose of the loan was seen as that of furnishing a means of consolidating the public debt and of strengthening the reserves of the central bank. The foreign exchange proceeds of the loan were turned over to the bank and, since the proceeds were in gold currencies, provided statutory cover for the sight liabilities of the bank. At the same time, the loan proceeds usually served as a counter-entry for the cancellation of part of the state's debt to the bank.[15] Thus, the loan served at one and the same time to reduce the public floating debt and thus the pressure on the Treasury; to increase the cover ratio of the bank and increase confidence in the bank's ability to maintain the announced parity; and to provide a mass of maneuver to cover temporary balance of payments deficits and to support the currency on the exchange market.

The credit, on the other hand, was extended by a group of central banks to the central bank of the stabilizing nation and was available to provide temporary assistance pending the issue of a loan. None of the four credits studied here, however, was actually used for this pur-

15 Part of the state debt was also canceled by the writing up of the bank's metallic and equivalent assets to the new parity level.

pose. Nevertheless, they did serve as psychological support for the currency and, more importantly, for the loan. In fact, the private bankers were usually unwilling to consider handling a loan issue unless it was coupled with a central bank credit which could be used as an indication to the market that the program had the blessing of responsible financial authorities. On the other hand, the central bankers made the extension of their assistance contingent upon a firm commitment for private banking support. There was, however, a second reason for the private bankers to insist upon the extension of a central bank credit. The central bankers were in a better position than the private bankers (the leaders of whom were usually the fiscal agents of the stabilizing governments) to insist upon essential conditions which would assure the success of the operation. In particular, the central bankers could demand the establishment of effective controls over the use of the loan proceeds and over the funds necessary to service the loan—measures that private bankers would find difficult to insist upon and almost impossible to enforce.

It is evident, however, that the central bankers were not a single entity as much of the above discussion implies. In each instance, the views of a number of different institutions had to be coordinated, or else the responsibility for negotiation had to be delegated to one or two of these institutions with the others more or less committed to accept the judgment of those institutions. So long as there was no institution strong enough to challenge the leadership of the Bank of England and the Federal Reserve Bank of New York, the second of these alternatives could be followed with no difficulty. The views of Benjamin Strong and Montagu Norman were so nearly identical and the two institutions worked in such close harmony that there was no serious division at the top. The others had no choice except to accept this leadership or remain outside of any consortium that might be formed. From early 1927, however, when the group of leaders expanded to three through the addition of the Bank of France, that group became too large for unity. Not only were there fundamental differences between the Bank of England and the Bank of France, but the unity of outlook on the part of the Bank of England and the Federal Reserve Bank of New York began to break down. Thus, the original unity of leadership disappeared, and at the same time no one of the three was strong enough alone to be accepted without question by the others as the leader. Without some form of unified leadership, effective executive action became difficult, if not impossible, in view of the problem of arriving at a common consensus of the views of ten or fifteen participating institutions.

It cannot be said that the Financial Committee of the League provided such unity of leadership for the central banks in the early 1920s since it operated in lieu of, not as part of, central bank action in support of postwar stabilization. But its stabilization activities did have a marked influence on central bank efforts in this field. The programs it developed for Austria and Hungary served as guides in judging the adequacy of other stabilization programs. In their essentials, these League programs provided for balancing of the state budget, establishment of an independent bank of issue with foreign advice, strict limitation on the availability of central bank credit for the government, and control of certain aspects of the national finances of the stabilizing nation through a Commissioner-General responsible to the League. It was recognized by the central bankers that some aspects of these programs might be unnecessary in certain cases. In particular, in the absence of hyper-inflation, controls could be eliminated or at least weakened. But it was precisely the problem of reaching agreement on the question of how much deviation from the League standard was justified in a specific case which gave rise to the difficulties among the central banks.

Chapter II. BELGIUM

Belgian postwar inflation stemmed from two principal sources: the redemption, at the end of the war, of German mark notes circulating in Belgium, and the regular budget deficits, which largely resulted from the decision of the government to assume the entire burden of rehabilitation. The mark conversion was rather ineptly handled in that the intention to convert at the prewar mint ratio of 1.25 francs to the mark was announced as early as November 9, 1918. The bulk of the conversion, however, was not accomplished until the following January. As a result of this delay between announcement and execution, it has been estimated that between 1 and 2 billion of the 6.109 billion marks converted were smuggled into Belgium after the public was aware of the planned conversion. Some of the conversion was effected through the sale of three-year bonds, but the bulk of it was financed by a 5.8-billion-franc advance from the National Bank to the government.[1] By the autumn of 1925, the state debt to the bank still stood at 5.68 billion francs.[2]

The total Belgian budget deficit over the years 1919–1926 amounted to 27.867 billion francs, of which only 650 million was attributable to the ordinary budget. The bulk of it was made up of extraordinary expenditures (11.536 billion francs) and amounts supposedly recoverable on reparation account (11.983 billion francs).[3] This aspect of the Belgian inflation was very similar, both

[1] Henry L. Shepherd, *The Monetary Experience of Belgium, 1914–1936* (Princeton, 1936), pp. 18–27. See also Fernand Baudhuin, *Histoire économique de la Belgique 1914–1939* (Bruxelles, 1944), I, pp. 122–23.

[2] Cable, October 6, 1925, Morgan Greenfell & Co. to J. P. Morgan & Co. Files of the Federal Reserve Bank of New York (hereafter cited as Federal Reserve). Correspondence, Banque Nationale de Belgique, May 1919–December 1925.

[3] Shepherd, *The Monetary Experience of Belgium, 1914–1936*, p. 29.

in cause and effect, to the French experience and was one factor in the similarity in postwar behavior of the two exchanges,[4] although reconstruction and relief expenditures probably loomed somewhat larger in overall Belgian public finances than they did in France. There were other similarities in the inflationary experience of the two nations. In neither case was there a complete loss of confidence in the national currency so that inflation never developed to runaway proportions. In fact, the velocity of circulation in both countries remained well below prewar until 1926.[5] This drop in velocity of circulation between 1913 and 1919 may have served to cushion the initial impact of immediate postwar money creation, particularly the Belgian mark conversion, and the fact that it rose slowly at least did little to aggravate the effects of the increasing note circulation and large floating debt. Until 1923, Belgian budget deficits could still be covered to a considerable degree by internal long-term borrowing. Thereafter, the government had to turn increasingly to short-term loans. Still, these took the form of public borrowing rather than of additional advances from the National Bank.[6]

Because of the relationship, at least in the public mind, between the Belgian and French francs, both Strong and Norman had some doubts about the advisability of attempts by the Belgians (as well as the Italians, who were in a somewhat similar position vis-à-vis the French franc) to stabilize independently of French stabilization. But significant changes in the Belgian situation began to develop in the summer of 1925. The Belgian elections of the spring of that year resulted in the resignation of the incumbent government. The So-

[4] *Ibid.*, p. 96. There were, of course, other causes for this solidarity of the two francs, both real and psychological. France accounted for a very large part of Belgian trade, both export and import, and the prewar parities of the two francs had, within the Latin Monetary Union, been identical. This tie within the Latin Monetary Union had not yet been formally broken so that, although both currencies were freely fluctuating at the time, there was a strong psychological tie between them.

[5] *Ibid.*, p. 74. Shepherd estimated the velocity of circulation in the two countries for the years 1919–1926 using both an index of industrial production and an index of agricultural production as a proxy for transactions in the equation $MV = PT$. Using industrial production, Belgian turnover (1913 = 100) rose from 33 in 1919 to 96 in 1926. French turnover, on the same basis, rose from 36 in 1919 to 100 in 1926. Using agricultural production, the corresponding Belgian figures are 49 and 79, the French 42 and 62.

[6] *Ibid.*, p. 36.

cialists gained in this election, but not sufficiently to control either branch of Parliament. As a result, there was some difficulty in forming a new government. After several abortive attempts by others, Viscount Poullet finally put together an acceptable coalition ministry on June 17, 1925. The Finance Ministry in this new cabinet went to Albert E. Janssen, who had been a director of the Belgian National Bank.[7] In a speech delivered at the London School of Economics on March 16, 1925, Janssen had indicated that there was no intention of stabilizing the franc in the near future and that official policy was to restore the franc, if not to prewar gold parity, at least to a parity considerably higher than that then prevailing.[8] Nevertheless, at the end of July, in the course of Strong's European trip in the summer of 1925, he and Norman visited Fernand Hautain, then Governor of the National Bank of Belgium, and the prospects for Belgian stabilization were discussed. The discussion was completely inconclusive, but Hautain was fairly optimistic about the prospects. The principal question concerned the debt settlement with the United States which was then under negotiation. Hautain felt that Janssen would be able to balance the budget for the next year provided that the American debt settlement was not too burdensome.[9]

This issue of debt settlement with the United States was significant, not only because of its impact on the Belgian budget, but also because a settlement would open up the American market to Belgian borrowing.[10] While debt settlement was only one of the conditions which Janssen considered essential before stabilization could

[7] *Ibid.*, pp. 129–30.

[8] *Ibid.*, p. 105. Baudhuin says that the immense majority of Belgian public opinion believed, at that time, that restoration to prewar parity was both desirable and possible (Baudhuin, *Histoire économique de la Belgique 1914–1939*, p. 156).

[9] Memorandum, "Discussions with Monsieur Hautain, Brussels, July 27, 28, 29, 1925," Strong Papers, European Trips.

[10] The reports of the United States Foreign Debt Commission make the problem clear: "Early in 1925, after much consideration, it was decided that it was contrary to the best interest of the United States to permit foreign governments which refused to adjust or make a reasonable effort to adjust their debts to the United States to finance any portion of their requirements in this country. States, municipalities, and private enterprises within the country concerned were included in the prohibition. Bankers consulting the State Department were notified that the Government objected to such financing" (United States, *Combined Annual Reports of the World War Foreign Debt Commission*, p. 39).

be attempted, the signature of the agreement on August 18, 1925, left only the attainment of budget equilibrium as a remaining precondition to be achieved. In presenting the budget estimates for 1926 to Parliament, Janssen said that three conditions were required before the monetary problem could be approached. First, solution of the reparations question, which was accomplished by the Dawes Plan. Second, solution of the problem of inter-Allied debts, which was accomplished by the Washington settlement with the United States. Third, equilibrium of the budget, which would be accomplished if the Parliament voted the emergency taxes asked of it.[11] The signature of the debt settlement agreement and the difficulties developing for the French franc in the summer of 1925—difficulties which seemed to offer some hope of breaking the tie between the Belgian and French francs—appear to have led Janssen to feel that there was some urgency in making a stabilization attempt at this time.

For a variety of reasons, the French franc had been depreciating through the summer of 1925. The slide was touched off by the public disclosure, in April of that year, that the note issue of the Bank of France had exceeded the legal maximum since December 1923 and that the published balance sheets of the bank had been designed deliberately to hide the fact.[12] As a result, the French franc fell approximately 10 per cent between April and July and it seems to have pulled the Belgian franc with it.[13] During the summer, both the French and the Belgians were negotiating a war debt settlement with the United States. Agreement was reached between the Belgians and the Americans in August 1925 on terms favorable to Belgium, whereas the negotiations with the French broke down in September. This, and the fact that a large bloc of the French public debt was maturing in December 1925,[14] promised to put the French franc under stronger pressure than the Belgian.

11 Shepherd, *The Monetary Experience of Belgium, 1914–1936*, p. 106.

12 Sir Cecil H. Kisch and W. A. Elkin, *Central Banks* (London, 1932), pp. 21–22.

13 The monthly low quotation for the Belgian franc also fell by about 10 per cent during this period, but the fall in the monthly high was not quite as rapid.

14 Cable, November 14, 1925, Strong to Anderson (Bank of England), Harrison Collection, Binder 13.

In any event, the Belgian National Bank began to intervene in support of the Belgian franc on September 15, 1925; and on September 28, 1925, Janssen called a meeting of Belgian bankers at which he announced his plans for stabilization. Presumably as a step toward limiting capital outflows, he asked the bankers to form a syndicate in order to sustain the domestic bond market. The syndicate was formed, although on a rather limited scale.[15] On October 5 Janssen, Hautain, and others visited Montagu Norman in London and discussed the Belgian stabilization program.[16] The next day, the Belgian party discussed their program with J. P. Morgan, whose firm was the United States financial agent for the Belgian government. Both Norman and Morgan were impressed by the argument that the present moment offered a unique opportunity to break the connection between the Belgian and French francs. In a cable that Morgan and Whitney sent to their New York office, they said: "They [the Belgians] say that unless this is done now, in view of the uncertainties attending the future in France, they may have much greater difficulty later on, which seems to Montague [sic] Norman and us, who all thought this was premature, a conclusive argument for prompt action." [17]

Janssen's plan was based on unduly optimistic estimates and had not been prepared with sufficient thoroughness. Its principal elements envisioned:

1. Stabilization based on gold at the rate of four new francs for one old.[18]

[15] Shepherd, *The Monetary Experience of Belgium, 1914–1936*, pp. 107–10. The syndicate provided only 60 million francs to be devoted to support of the market.

[16] Norman immediately cabled Strong, and his cable indicates that it was the breakdown in Franco-American debt negotiations which was the factor most effective in convincing him that there was a possibility of breaking the Belgian-French franc tie: "Since our conversation in Brussels situation may have been altered by failure of Caillaux to reach settlement in Washington which may lead to depreciation of French franc and so endanger recent stability of Belgian franc" (cable, October 5, 1925, Norman to Strong, Harrison Collection, Binder 13).

[17] Cable, October 6, 1925, Morgan and Whitney from Morgan Greenfell & Co. to Denkstein, J. P. Morgan & Co., Federal Reserve, Correspondence, Banque Nationale de Belgique, May 1919–December 1925.

[18] Strong immediately questioned this ratio on the basis of the New York impression that Belgian prices were relatively low (cable, October 6, 1925, Strong to Norman, Harrison Collection, Binder 13).

2. A foreign loan of $150 to $160 million, of which $100 million would have to be raised in the United States.

3. A balanced budget for 1926. Only 400 million francs of new taxes were envisioned, however, and no serious reduction in expenditures planned. Principal reliance seems to have been placed on collecting tax arrears from previous years and increasing the receipts from existing taxes. It is not clear how Janssen expected to achieve these results.

4. Writing up the gold and equivalent assets of the National Bank to the new exchange rate. The resulting profits, along with the proceeds of the foreign loan, would be used to reduce the state debt to the bank from 5.680 to 1.600 billion francs. There was no provision, however, for reduction of the internal floating debt outside the bank.

5. Bank capital to be raised by public stock issue from 50 million to 200 million francs.

6. Renewal of the Bank's charter for a thirty-year period.[19]

On being advised of the London meetings, Strong immediately called a conference with New York bankers and, on October 8, 1925, cabled Norman his impression of their reactions. The factors that were to be the stumbling blocks for the Janssen attempt already were evident. Strong's impression of the principal difficult points were:

(a) Size of loan following two large Belgian issues so recently.[20]
(b) Failure to balance budget as expected under legislation promised at time of former loans.
(c) Size of foreign payments required for service of external debts after funding with U.S. Government and placing this loan.
(d) Indefinite nature of plans for increased revenue and for maintaining balance of external payments.
(e) Size of internal floating debt and early maturities.[21]

[19] Memorandum of October 5, 1925 meeting prepared by Norman and contained in cable, October 6, 1925, from Morgan Greenfell & Co. to J. P. Morgan & Co., Federal Reserve, Correspondence, Banque Nationale de Belgique, May 1919–December 1925.

[20] The Belgian government had floated two bond issues in the United States of $50 million each in December 1924 and January 1925 (Shepherd, *The Monetary Experience of Belgium, 1914–1936*, p. 66).

[21] Cable, October 8, 1925, Strong to Norman, Harrison Collection, Binder 13.

It was already evident that considerable time would be required to negotiate a long-term loan of the size desired. As an interim measure, the Belgian Finance Minister, the National Bank of Belgium, the Bank of England, and a group of private banks, which included J. P. Morgan and Company, signed a credit agreement in London on October 16, 1925. The agreement provided a $27.5-million revolving credit to the Belgian government against Belgian Dollar Treasury Bills.[22] On the basis of this credit, Janssen announced that "agreement in principle" had been reached with the bankers; however, this again seems to have involved some wishful thinking on Janssen's part. Certainly, the bankers—at least Morgan—were eager to help,[23] but there were too many open questions for them to agree at this time to handle a long-term loan or to pass final judgment on the prospects for the plan. Since the primary problem with respect to the loan issue lay in its acceptability to the American market, Hautain, Van Zeeland (Secretary of the National Bank of Belgium), and Vandevyvere (Belgian Minister of Agriculture) went to New York to continue the discussions.

The New York discussions centered on the issue of how budgetary balance was to be attained since the bankers were unwilling to consider a bond issue without satisfactory assurances on this point. In particular, they mistrusted the Belgian government's confidence in its ability to collect back taxes, a measure on which the achievement of budgetary balance depended so heavily. In addition, Strong expressed dissatisfaction to Hautain with the way the National Bank had so far handled credit policy.[24] Strong felt that the National Bank should have immediately raised bank rate and rationed credit. Having failed to do so, the bank had lost almost a billion francs of reserves and the demand for exchange was fed in part by the bank's own advances to the market. Besides the uncertainties in the Belgian

22 Cable, October 17, 1925, Norman to Strong, *ibid.*

23 The Morgan and Whitney cable of October 6, 1925, said: ". . . feel that it is of such great importance to the United States, and the world in general, to add to the number of gold basis countries, that we should make every effort to satisfy Belgian requirements since we are their agents and believe in what they are trying to do" (Federal Reserve, Correspondence, Banque Nationale de Belgique, May 1919–December 1925).

24 Cable, November 14, 1925, Strong to Anderson (then Deputy Governor of the Bank of England), Harrison Collection, Binder 13.

situation, there were doubts about the ability of the American market to absorb a bond issue as large as $100 million.[25] By November 27, 1925, J. P. Morgan and Company and the Guaranty Trust Company had taken a firm position that it was impossible to give an immediate commitment with respect to the bond issue. As an alternative, it was suggested that the private bank credit be doubled and extended for one year. Strong cabled this suggestion to the Bank of England and offered, if the enlarged private credit could be arranged, to take up to $5 million of bills from the National Bank of Belgium and to continue purchases for that amount for a maximum of one year. The offer was contingent upon other central banks taking an aggregate like amount. Strong's cable went on to say: "The bankers must thereafter reach some conclusion as to the budget and the bond issue with such necessary deliberation as the subject demands. We will not however make our action contingent upon this." [26]

The Bank of England, in conjunction with the National Banks of the Netherlands and Switzerland, agreed to provide the other $5 million. The Swiss Bank, however, required that the credit be closed out not later than March 31, and it was agreed that all should set the same conditions.[27] When agreement was reached on the private and central bank credits, Hautain and his party returned to Belgium. The central bank credits, however, never became effective because of delay in providing the National Bank of Belgium with legal authority to guarantee bills rediscounted abroad. Probably the Belgians also saw little point in pressing the issue unless the prospects of pushing through the entire program improved.[28] But the

[25] The fact that J. P. Morgan & Co. headed a syndicate which announced, on November 20, 1925, the issue of a $100-million Italian stabilization loan may have had some bearing on the matter. Not only was there the question of the market's ability to absorb two such foreign issues, but the experience with the Italian issue was not encouraging. It was heavily oversubscribed by banking and investment houses, but the public was slow to buy. By March 1926, a considerable amount of the bonds remained unsold to the public (Shepherd, *The Monetary Experience of Belgium, 1914–1936*, pp. 125–26).

[26] Cable, November 27, 1925, Strong to Norman and Anderson, Harrison Collection, Binder 13.

[27] Cable, December 2, 1925, Norman to Strong, *ibid.*

[28] In a letter of February 5, 1926, to Strong, Norman said: ". . . there can be no question of the credit being drawn upon until the amendment to Article 8 of the Bank Law has been passed by the Belgian Parliament and has received

principle of joint central bank credit extensions had been established.

Loan negotiations were resumed in early March 1926 in Brussels
and in London. The private bankers, however, were unwilling to
consider a loan larger than $100 million ($50 million each in the
United States and in Europe) and then only for a period of three
years. There was some discussion of the possibility of central bank
credits for a period of three years making up the remaining $50 mil-
lion, but it was evident that a three-year loan would mature too
soon to serve the required purpose. In any event, pessimistic rumors
reached Brussels concerning the London negotiations and provoked
a new demand for foreign exchange. Finally on March 15, 1926,
after the Belgians had put $107 million on the market in the period
September 15–March 15, support of the franc was withdrawn. Janssen did not immediately admit that his plan had failed and continued negotiations with the bankers. But he was finally forced into re-
signing on May 7, 1926, and the entire Poullet cabinet fell on May 9.

From the point of view of the central bankers, the Janssen attempt left three legacies. First, the bankers were confirmed in their
suspicion that a conversion ratio anywhere near the order of 4 to 1
could not be sustained. Since the principal source of the breakdown
of the Janssen stabilization attempt was the unrealistic assumptions
as to how budget balance could be achieved in 1926, the Janssen effort did not actually represent a realistic test of the 4-to-1 exchange
ratio. Nevertheless, the experience left the central bankers more
willing than they otherwise might have been to accept, indeed to
welcome, a conversion ratio of 7 to 1. Second, the experience destroyed the bankers' confidence in Hautain. In a letter of September
11, 1926, to Pierre Jay, Strong wrote:

Elaborating the point about the management of the Bank: very confidentially, I haven't confidence in Hautain. I can't say that he deceived us
when he was in New York; I am pretty certain that he did not give us all
essential information, notwithstanding repeated requests for it. He never

---

the Royal Assent" (Strong Papers, Bank of England). Most published works indicate that the credit was not consummated because of the failure of the long-
term loan. But the credit was not contingent upon agreement on the loan and,
in fact, was designed to provide time for further loan negotiations.

carried out his promise to keep us informed by mail, and I learn from Mr. Osborne of the Bank here [of England] that the response which he gets to requests for information which had been definitely pledged in connection with the credits arranged six months ago is unsatisfactory and incomplete, and he still feels that he is without adequate information. If Hautain is not to continue as head of the Bank, someone must be satisfied as to his successor. We are not in position to satisfy ourselves directly, and that question, I think, should squarely be put up to Governor Norman and the bankers. . . . We must be very careful not to get into the position of dictating or controlling the situation in such a way that if anything goes wrong Francqui can say that he was coerced by the foreign bankers. . . . Of course the chief danger would be that we would be charged with insisting upon a change in the governorship of the Bank. I cannot imagine anything worse than to have the charge made that we were responsible for such occurrences. In fact, I feel this so strongly I would almost be willing to go ahead without any change in the Bank rather than take any risk in that respect.[29]

Third, the Bank of England and the Federal Reserve Bank of New York had developed a certain proprietary feeling about Belgian stabilization. That the Bank of France was not consulted at this time was only natural. Not only had France not yet stabilized, even *de facto*, but she was monetarily so weak as to be a likely candidate to ask for, rather than to give, assistance. But the practice of bilateral dealing between the Anglo-Saxon banks continued at a time when the impact on French sensibilities could be more serious.

After the fall of the Poullet cabinet, there was again some difficulty in forming a new Belgian government. Finally, on May 17, 1926, Henri Jaspar undertook the task and, three days later, announced his National Union cabinet. The dominant figure in the ministry was Émile Francqui, whose announced sole purpose in accepting a position in it was to accomplish monetary reform. Since he did not consider himself a man of politics, he refused to accept a portfolio and, indeed, he retired from the government two weeks after promulgation of the stabilization decree. But, for the few months that he was in power, he provided the forceful leadership that was essential if order was to be brought out of the chaos. Even so, order did not come immediately.

[29] Letter, September 11, 1926, Strong to Jay, Federal Reserve, Correspondence, National Bank of Belgium, March 1926–October 1926.

According to Francqui, between the time of the March abandonment of franc support and the accession to power of the Jaspar Ministry, 634 million additional francs had had to be raised by money creation. At the moment that the Jaspar Ministry took the reins, Treasury bonds were being redeemed at the rate of 25 million francs daily. The total state debt to the National Bank was 6.5 billion francs and growing. The internal floating debt outside the bank of 6 billion francs was reimbursable at various dates, all before December 31, 1926. In addition, there was an external floating debt equivalent to almost 2 billion francs. The Jaspar Ministry immediately instituted a series of economy measures and passed new tax laws designed to add about 1.5 billion francs annually to state revenues.[30] Half of the private bankers' credit extended to the Janssen Treasury had expired at the end of March and the other half was due to expire on June 30, 1926. Only about $13 million of this was actually in use, however, and the bankers agreed to extend this amount for another three months.[31]

These measures alone were not enough to counteract the fall of the Belgian franc, now aggravated by the simultaneous flight from the French franc. The high point of the crisis was reached on July 12, 1926, when the Belgian franc fell to a low of 2.115 United States cents. As a result of the disaster of that day, Francqui was able to get a bill through Parliament on July 16 granting the government *plein pouvoir* to deal with matters of financial improvement and the preparation of monetary stabilization. The power was limited to a period of six months; but within that period the government could deal with these matters by decree. The impact of the passage of this law was enough in itself to bring on an immediate improvement in the strength of the Belgian franc.

The next measure in the Francqui reforms was undertaken, however, by passage of law rather than by decree. This was the only step in the following stabilization actions that was not accomplished by decree, but it had such far-reaching consequences that Francqui apparently felt that it should be acted upon by Parliament. This step was the conversion of the State Railways into the Belgian National

[30] Shepherd, *The Monetary Experience of Belgium, 1914–1936*, pp. 147–51.
[31] Letter, June 22, 1926, Harrison to Strong, Strong Papers, Harrison to Strong, 1926–27.

Railway Company. The purpose of the measure was not to relieve the budget of railway deficits, although these deficits had been a burden on state finances for some time. The primary purpose, however, was to effect a forced conversion of the internal floating debt. The company was capitalized at 11 billion francs—1 billion in ordinary shares, which went to the state, and 10 billion in preferred shares. Voting rights were so distributed that control remained with the government. The law provided that the preferred shares were to be issued on a preferential basis to holders of long- and short-term public debt. Although the terms on which the shares were issued were adequate to make them attractive to the market, holders of maturing public debt were virtually forced to convert. By decree of July 31, 1926, the right of redemption of all 6-month Treasury bills and of 5-year Treasury bonds maturing December 1, 1926, was rescinded. The remaining alternative for the bill and bond holders was to convert these securities into railway company shares. A special provision was made for bills and maturing bonds held by banks in order to avoid putting the banks into an illiquid position. But the majority of the securities were held by the general public, and about 75 per cent of the short-term public debt was converted by this operation into railway company shares. The balance was converted into bonds with somewhat more deferred maturity.[32]

One of the factors that made the railway company shares attractive was that dividend payments and redemption of principal was guaranteed at a rate of 175 francs to the pound sterling. Although this was the rate at which stabilization was finally effected, it is not clear whether the guarantee was set at this rate because Francqui had already settled on this rate for stabilization or whether, when the time came to select the stabilization rate, this guarantee played a decisive role in the choice.[33]

The effect of these energetic measures—and, it must be recognized, similar measures taking place in France at the same time—on

32 Shepherd, *The Monetary Experience of Belgium, 1914–1936,* pp. 156–61.

33 There are indications, however, that Francqui had already made up his mind to stabilize at this rate. Strong wrote Harrison from Amsterdam, August 9, 1926, saying: "I also gather from Francqui that he has about fixed his mind on stabilization at the ratio of 7 to 1, which is about 175 francs to the pound, and roughly 36 francs to the dollar" (Federal Reserve, Correspondence, National Bank of Belgium, March 1926–October 1926).

the Belgian franc was such that, by September, it had reached the rate of 175 to the pound. There had as yet been no request for further foreign assistance and, in fact, even the Belgian National Bank had been left on the sidelines. Strong, in a letter of August 3, 1926, to Harrison, wrote: "From Vissering [Governor of the Netherlands National Bank] I learn that he [Francqui] is not on speaking terms with Hautain. They have not seen each other since Francqui took office, nor for some time before, and the National Bank apparently is entirely out of touch with what is being done." [34] Thus, it appeared that the central bankers would not have to raise the issue of dissatisfaction with the management of the National Bank of Belgium. Louis Franck replaced Hautain as Governor just before the October 1926 London negotiations, which were conducted for the Belgians by Francqui and Franck.

By mid-September, the internal floating debt had been consolidated; the foreign short-term loans either paid or extended; extraordinary revenues had been voted to meet the service charges on the public debt; and economies and reforms had been introduced into the government administration. Even without a foreign loan, the prospects for Belgian stabilization looked much brighter than they had the previous year. But Francqui still wanted the foreign loan as a means of reducing the state's debt to the bank, of strengthening the bank's exchange reserves, and as an indication of international confidence. As a result, he again approached the bankers about re-opening negotiations for a loan of $100 million. A meeting to discuss the matter was held at the Bank of England on September 14, 1926, with Norman and Osborne of the Bank of England, Strong of the Federal Reserve Bank of New York, and representatives of a large number of private banking houses present. The conferees agreed that Mr. Ter Meulen of Hope and Company, Amsterdam, and Mr. Du Bois of the Swiss Banking Corporation would see Francqui in a few days and tell him:

1. That there would be no loans or credits arranged by the bankers for the purpose of stabilization unless the central banks were satisfied to extend a credit also to the National Bank;

[34] Letter, August 3, 1926, Strong to Harrison, Strong Papers, European Trips.

2. That the amount of the long-term loan should be kept as small as possible to meet the requirements of the National Bank for reserve, and that any additional amount should be in the form of credits to the Government for a period so as to avoid heavy foreign debt service;

3. That "de jure" stabilization should take place at once that the plan was worked out and effective.[35]

The central bankers, however, were as yet unwilling to commit themselves, even in principle, to a credit extension to the Belgian National Bank. Strong discussed the attitude of the Federal Reserve Bank of New York at this same September 14 meeting. After pointing out the danger of entrusting a stabilization program such as the one under discussion to changing finance ministers and that, therefore, such a program should be entrusted to the National Bank, he went on to say:

If the National Bank were to be entrusted with the program and it was a "sine qua non" that we should extend credits to the National Bank before loans could be made, I would, before [being] willing to recommend such credits, wish to know about the condition of the Bank, what M. Francqui proposed in the way of reorganization, what effect the plan of stabilization would have upon the statement and affairs of the Bank, and what he contemplated in the matter of management and direction. Therefore, I was unable without more information and without consultation to make any statement as to what we would do.[36]

Francqui and Franck visited London, October 2–4, 1926, to press for the loan and credit. Besides giving technical details of the impact of the stabilization plan on the National Bank, Franck indicated to Norman and Strong that:

1. Prior to the issue of any loan, the entire Belgian external floating debt would be paid off from valuta now in the hands of the government and the bank.

2. As soon as possible after the necessary loans and credits had been obtained, it was the intention of the Belgian government to undertake de jure stabilization.

3. The rate of stabilization could not be fixed until the moment

35 Memorandum of meeting held at the Bank of England, September 14, 1926, to discuss Belgian Stabilization, Strong Papers, European Trips 1926, Vol. 2.
36 Ibid.

of stabilization, when it would be decided in conference between the government and the bank.[37]

Despite the uncertainties concerning the rate of stabilization and its timing that Franck's statement entailed, the New York Federal Reserve Bank, the Bank of England, the Reichsbank, and the National Bank of Holland had already agreed to the extension of a credit by October 3, 1926. In addition, the National Banks of Switzerland and Hungary had tentatively agreed to take part. The credit was to be for one year in the amount of £5 million and was to be conditional on a private bankers' loan or credit of not less than £15 million to the Belgian government.[38] Franck was advised of this agreement in principle by a letter from Norman dated October 5, 1926. Enclosed with the letter was a memorandum from Strong in which, among other things, Strong pointed out that both the bankers handling the government loan and those extending credits would need assurances as to the justification for the new value of the franc. But he also asserted that the responsibility for setting that rate rested with the government and could not be shared by foreign bankers.[39]

In all this time, the Bank of France had apparently been left out of the picture although it was aware, of course, of the fact that the negotiations were going on and had had some discussions with representatives of Morgan's. It was not even asked to participate in the credit until mid-October when Pierre Quesnay visited London. On his return, October 14, 1926, he advised Moreau of the credit agreement and of the fact that the National Banks of Austria, Sweden, and Japan had been added to the list of those which had expressed an interest in participating. Norman, through Quesnay, pressed the importance of the cooperation of the Bank of France in the effort.[40]

[37] Memorandum, October 6, 1926, covering Franck's London visit, Federal Reserve, Correspondence, National Bank of Belgium, March 1926–October 1926.

[38] Cable, October 3, 1926, Jay to Strong, Harrison Collection, Binder 33.

[39] Letter, October 5, 1926, Norman to Franck with enclosed memorandum, Federal Reserve, Correspondence, National Bank of Belgium, March 1926–October 1926.

[40] Moreau, *Souvenirs*, pp. 129–30. Moreau had to consult his government before replying. Poincaré agreed to French participation, but Moreau added in his diary, "En tout cas, il voudrait que nous subordonnions notre concours à l'octroi de concessions douanières par la Belgique." [In any case, he would like

While Moreau's diary reflects no pique at this time over what might be considered a slight to the Bank of France, the fact that the only banks which were firmly committed at this point were the very ones which he considered under Norman's influence [41] did nothing to allay his fundamental mistrust of Norman.[42] In any event, the Bank of France did agree to participate in the credit in an amount equal to the participation of the Reichsbank, itself perhaps some indication of a reluctance to have the Bank of France considered in any way inferior to the Reichsbank.

The negotiations for the central bank credit almost got snagged on a technical problem between the Federal Reserve Bank and the other participants. In the early negotiations, it was agreed that the participating banks would charge a commission of 0.5 per cent on the credit and that the interest charged on any credits drawn would be 1 per cent above the prevailing bank rate of the bank extending the credit, but in no case would the interest charged be less than 6 per cent. The Federal Reserve Bank of New York, and more partic-

---

our agreement to be dependent upon the granting of customs concessions by Belgium.] Events obviously moved too rapidly to follow up this thought.

[41] Moreau specifically mentions that Strong of the Federal Reserve, Vissering of the National Bank of Holland, and Schacht of the Reichsbank were under Norman's influence (ibid., p. 137).

[42] After his first meeting with Norman, Moreau wrote in his diary, "Il est impérialiste, voulant pour son pays qu'il aime passionnément la domination du monde. Toutes ses combinaisons monétaires ont pour but de faire du sterling l'instrument d'échange universel" (ibid., p. 49). [He is an imperialist seeking world domination for his country, which he loves passionately. The goal of all of his monetary arrangements is to make sterling the universal instrument of exchange.]

Moreau found Norman's idea that central bank cooperation among banks independent of their governments might lift monetary problems out of the political domain somewhat doctrinaire, undoubtedly utopian, and perhaps even Machiavelian (ibid., p. 137). Nor was this mistrust peculiar with Moreau. Strong commented in a letter to Pierre Jay on the suspicion of the political motives in the relations between Norman and Schacht prevalent in France and Italy and, Strong suspected, in Belgium as well. He goes on to say: "I have been strongly advised, both from inside and outside, that if we go ahead with participation in any stabilization plans in any of these three countries, we should not do it through Governor Norman as an intermediary. They seem to be afraid of him and somewhat mistrust him, not as to his integrity or reliability or anything of that sort, but I think they feel that he is at times too able for them and that he is not as disinterested as we are. I don't think any feeling of that sort exists as to the Federal Reserve Bank or myself" (letter, September 11, 1926, Strong to Jay, Federal Reserve, Correspondence, National Bank of Belgium, March 1926–October 1926).

ularly the Federal Reserve Board in Washington, felt that the minimum interest charge should be no higher than 5 per cent and that no commission should be charged by the Federal Reserve since the Federal Reserve stabilization credit to the Bank of England, on which no commission was charged, was still outstanding. When Norman was advised of this, he was taken aback. In a letter of October 20, 1926, to Harrison, he pointed out that when Strong had been in Europe the past summer, he had told Norman that he would never again grant a central bank credit without charging a moderate commission. According to Norman, this view agreed with that of the Continental central bankers, but not with his own. Norman went on to say:

Imagine, therefore my surprise to find you in the position of a protagonist for charging no commission! Am I on my head or my heels? Please talk to Strong and Jay and some day let me know which of the two and what to do.

We shall get out of the present impasse, I presume, by all the participants charging a commission and by your repaying yours to the National Bank of Belgium. Not a very fine example of unanimity!

The second is a high minimum rate of interest. The object of a high minimum is to protect Franck against the Belgian Bankers, the Belgian public and the Belgian Government; to help him to feel and know and say that, having to pay a high rate of interest (plus a commission) if he borrows our money, he obviously cannot reduce his Bank Rate below 7% or 8% (whatever it is) during the currency of his credit. I consider that for these reasons a high minimum was vital . . .

If we thus admit the need for a high rate, need we dispute whether the minimum should be 5%, 6%, or 7%? In Europe nobody can admit that 5% is a high rate: as a minimum (that is a 4% Bank rate) it would be unlikely to be operative under this credit. On the other hand, 7% does seem to be a high rate even in Europe; it would probably force the Belgian Bank to maintain right along a Bank Rate of 8% or more. The proper rate has therefore seemed empirically to work out at 6% as a minimum (that is a Bank Rate of 5%), and I am extremely sorry that your friends in Washington have not seen their way to accept this apparently reasonable suggestion.[43]

It is interesting to note Norman's view of the interest charge as a constraint on Belgian monetary policy. It was a form of control that

[43] Letter, October 20, 1926, Norman to Harrison, *ibid.*

could be effective even if, as was the case, the credit was not drawn upon. It was a view with which Strong must certainly have agreed, but the Federal Reserve authorities of the time, including Strong, apparently were concerned about leaving the impression that they were in any sense discriminating against Belgium in the terms attached to the credit. In the case of the credits later extended to other nations, this question did not arise since the British credit had by then expired. Still, there was a certain inconsistency in the fact that Strong *et al.* accepted without question a 6 per cent minimum in the Polish and Italian negotiations while the Belgian credit remained open.[44]

In any case, the solution ultimately adopted for Belgium was that which Norman had foreseen. A special clause was inserted in the agreement setting the interest rate at 6 per cent minimum except that, in the case of the Federal Reserve Bank of New York, the minimum would be 5 per cent. The commission was paid and that portion of it paid to the Federal Reserve Bank of New York which covered the period that the credit to the Bank of England was still open (to May 14, 1927) was refunded to the National Bank of Belgium.[45]

The contracts for a $100-million, thirty-year, 7 per cent bond issue were signed with the private bankers on October 23, 1926.[46] The central bank credit, originally for $25 million, became effective Oc-

---

[44] It must be recognized, on the other hand, that the Belgian credit expired at the end of October 1927, only days after the Polish credit became effective and before the Italian one went into effect.

[45] Letter, May 19, 1927, Harrison to the Governors of the other Federal Reserve Banks, Federal Reserve, Correspondence, National Bank of Belgium, March 1926–October 1926.

[46] Issued as follows:

United States	$50,000,000
England	£7,250,000
Holland	£1,250,000
Switzerland	Sw. Fr. 32,000,000
Sweden	kr. 9,000,000

The issue was made at 94 and was redeemable at 105. The net proceeds to the Belgian government, after allowing for the reduced issue price, commissions, and costs, was approximately $90 million (Prospectus for the London issue of the loan, Federal Reserve, Correspondence, National Bank of Belgium, Revolving Credit [Eff Oct. 25, 1926], and Shepherd, *The Monetary Experience of Belgium, 1914–1936*, p. 166).

tober 25, 1926, when the stabilization decree was issued.[47] Stabilization was at a rate of 175 Belgian francs to the British pound, or 2.781 United States cents to the franc.

It is today generally agreed that this exchange ratio considerably undervalued the Belgian franc. Indeed, a marked rise in Belgian prices, as compared with world prices, occurred in the years following 1926. The wholesale price indices for the United States, United Kingdom, and Belgium for the years 1926, 1929 (peak of Belgian price inflation), and 1931 (the year of British suspension of gold payments) are as follows: [48]

Year	United States	United Kingdom	Belgium
1926	143	148	744
1929	138	137	851
1931	106	105	626

Between 1926 and 1929, the United States index fell 3.5 per cent, the British fell 7.4 per cent, and the Belgian rose 14.4 per cent. Between 1926 and 1931, the United States index fell 26 per cent, the British 29 per cent, and the Belgian only 16 per cent.

[47] Original participants were

Austria	£500,000
England	£1,000,000
France	£1,000,000
Germany	Mks 20,000,000
Holland	Fls 12,000,000
Hungary	£500,000
Japan	£500,000
Sweden	Kr. 5,000,000
United States	$10,000,000

Later, the Bank of Italy (10,000,000 gold lire) and the National Bank of Switzerland (Sw. Fr. 5,000,000) joined the group, adding approximately $3,000,000 (cable, November 25, 1926, Bank of England to the Federal Reserve Bank of New York, Federal Reserve, Correspondence, National Bank of Belgium, March 1926–October 1926).

[48] Data are taken from the *Statistical Yearbook of the League of Nations 1930/31* (Geneva, 1931), pp. 270–72, and the same yearbook for 1935/36, pp. 239–41. The indices for the United States and the United Kingdom for 1926 and 1929 are on a 1913 base of 100. The figures for 1931 were given on a 1929 base and have been adjusted to the 1913 base. The Belgian indices for 1926 and 1929 are on a 1914 base of 100. The 1931 figure was given on a 1929 base and has been adjusted to the 1914 base.

A similar comparison can be made on the basis of a cost of living index. The data are as follows: [49]

Year	United States	United Kingdom	Belgium
1926	166	170	174
1929	162	163	216
1931	142	147	201

Between 1926 and 1929, the United States and British indices fell 2.4 and 4.1 per cent respectively, whereas the Belgain index rose 24.1 per cent. Between 1926 and 1931, the United States and British indices fell 14.5 and 13.5 per cent, while the Belgian rose 15.5 per cent.

Thus, the post-stabilization price behavior clearly indicates that the franc was indeed undervalued at 2.781 United States cents. But, can the experience tell us anything about approximately what the appropriate level would have been? On the assumption that the 1913 exchange ratio of 19.3 United States cents to the franc was an equilibrium rate [50] and using United States prices as a proxy for world prices, a purchasing power parity calculation for the year 1929 using wholesale prices gives a level of 3.13 United States cents for the franc. This indicates an undervaluation of about 11 per cent for the franc. A similar calculation using British prices as a proxy for world prices gives a percentage figure of 12. Similar calculations for the year 1931 give an undervaluation of about 25 per cent using United States prices and about 15 per cent using British prices.

Similar calculations using a cost of living index are more difficult since the Belgian index is not carried back to the prewar years. If it is assumed, however, that the Belgian cost of living rose from 1913 to 1921 (the earliest year for which an index is available) by the same percentage as Belgian wholesale prices rose in that period, the index can be carried back to 1913. A purchasing power parity calcu-

[49] Sources are again the *Statistical Yearbook of the League of Nations 1930/31*, pp. 274–76, and the same yearbook for 1935/36, pp. 242–44. The 1926 and 1929 figures for the United States and the United Kingdom are on a 1914 base of 100. The Belgian base for comparable years is 1921 = 100. All 1931 figures were given on a 1929 base and have been adjusted to the appropriate base so as to be comparable with the 1926 and 1929 data.

[50] And ignoring the slight difference in base year of the indices.

lation on this basis yields the following percentages of undervaluation of the Belgian franc:

World Price Proxy	1929	1931
United States index	29.6%	25.3%
United Kingdom index	43.1%	38.6%

The difficulties inherent in attempting to apply the purchasing power parity theory are too well known to require repetition here. In addition to all the usual problems, the post-1926 period was sufficiently unsettled to make international price level comparisons extremely suspect. The terminal dates of 1929 and 1931 have been selected here precisely because of the major economic and financial changes that took place in those years. In addition to representing the peak of Belgian price inflation, the year 1929 also represents, of course, the start of the world slide into the Great Depression. In view of this latter consideration, it would be desirable to terminate the period of comparison here. There is considerable doubt, however, whether the period from the last quarter of 1926 through 1929 was long enough to permit Belgian prices to adjust fully to the new exchange ratio.

British suspension of gold payments in 1931, on the other hand, changed the situation so radically that calculations beyond that year have little meaning. Even the years 1930 and 1931 can be logically included in the comparison only if one makes the assumption that the impact of the price declines that began in 1929 on Belgian, United States, and United Kindom prices was approximately the same. On the basis of this assumption, it would appear that Belgian wholesale prices had fully adjusted by 1929. Between that year and 1931, United States and United Kingdom wholesale prices dropped about 23 per cent, whereas Belgian wholesale prices fell 26 per cent. Retail prices, as represented by a cost of living index, do not seem to have fully adjusted by 1929. The United States cost of living index fell 12 per cent between 1929 and 1931, the United Kingdom index fell 10 per cent, and the Belgian only 7 per cent.

Despite the difficulties involved in interpreting the results, there is a clear indication of undervaluation of the Belgian franc by at least 12 per cent (based upon wholesale prices and the assumption of complete adjustment by 1929). If, however, one drops the latter assumption or uses a cost of living index with terminal dates of either 1929 or 1931, the undervaluation was at least of the order of 25 per cent.

It should also be remembered that the above calculations are *ex post*, whereas Norman and Strong had to consider the problem *ex ante*. As early as February 11, 1926, Norman wrote Strong that "the ratio is still undecided, but like yourself I mistrust the 4 to 1 or even 107 to the £ (4.52 cents to Fc. 1) as too favourable to Belgium." It is interesting to note that "too favourable" meant to Norman an overvaluation, not an undervaluation, of the franc.[51] In other words, he adopted a terms of trade, rather than a balance of payments, measure of what is favorable or unfavorable. His attitude tended to encourage balance of payments difficulties for Britain—really a strange view for a central banker to take.[52] But it was a view that was consistent with Norman's and Strong's propensity to view the exchange rate problem solely in the light of the capability of the stabilizing nation to maintain the chosen rate.

Included with Norman's letter was a study prepared by the Bank of England that predicted a rise of Belgian internal prices of 12 to 18 per cent if the franc were stabilized at 107 to the pound.[53] But both Norman and Strong consistently adopted the point of view that the choice of exchange rate was a matter solely for the stabilizing nation to decide. In addition, this letter was written prior to the failure of the Janssen attempt. Norman and Strong apparently assigned a greater importance to the role of the choice of conversion ratio in this failure than seems to have been justified. As a result,

---

[51] A 4-to-1 conversion resulted in a value of 4.82 cents for the franc, which Norman obviously considered more favorable to Belgium than a value of 4.52 cents for the franc.

[52] Norman's view is, of course, explicable in part at least by his concern for the financial interests of the City and for sterling's position in the financing of international trade. Still, the potential difficulty for British balance of payments was aggravated by the fact that, as Clarke points out, "On the Continent, in contrast, there was less preoccupation with financial status and more with the need to maintain or strengthen the international competitive position of trade and industry" (Clarke, *Central Bank Cooperation: 1924–31*, p. 20).

[53] Letter, February 11, 1926, Norman to Strong, and enclosed memorandum, Strong Papers, Bank of England.

they raised no question about Francqui's conversion ratio of 7 to 1. Even without the Janssen experience, however, it is quite possible that they would not have questioned a 7-to-1 ratio since they obviously considered a move toward undervaluation to be unfavorable to Belgium.

In any case, the rate chosen for stabilization was, in itself, enough to ease the strain of Belgian stabilization. Not only was it low enough to permit Belgium to compete on favorable terms on foreign markets (at least until Belgian internal prices readjusted to this new rate), but the fact that it was set relatively low [54] permitted that much more of a writing up of the value of the metallic and equivalent assets of the National Bank. The resulting paper profits, as well as the proceeds of the foreign loan, served to strengthen the bank's cover against its sight liabilities as well as to reduce the state debt to the bank from 6.705 billion to 2 billion francs.

Stabilization was also assisted by the recovery of the French franc and its *de facto* stabilization at a higher rate than that of the Belgian franc (approximately 125 French francs to the British pound). The fact that this rate for the French franc was already well above that for the Belgian franc may well have assisted Émile Moreau in resisting pressure to permit a further rise in the exchange value of the French franc. In any event, the rate relationship between the two francs was such as to ease the immediate strain of Belgian stabilization.

Finally, the British coal strike lasted from May to November of 1926 with the result that there was a great increase in the production and export of Belgian coal. The peak in production was reached in December 1926, and production began to fall and inventories to rise from January 1927.[55] Nevertheless, the British strike was a marked aid in the critical period.

[54] As in the case of France, the rate could only be maintained through heavy purchases of foreign exchange by the National Bank of Belgium. There seems to be general agreement among students of Belgian monetary history that, in the long run, the low exchange rate was damaging to Belgium in permitting postponement of needed structural adjustments. See Shepherd, *The Monetary Experience of Belgium, 1914–1936*, p. 186; Baudhuin, *Histoire économique de la Belgique 1914–1939*, p. 173; Hugo Cats, *Les effets du nouveau régime monétaire en Belgique sur son économie, depuis la stabilisation jusqu'a la crise économique* (Anvers, 1933), pp. 24–25; J. de Longeaux, *Conséquences économiques de la stabilisation Belge* (Paris, 1928), p. 115.

[55] Longeaux, *Conséquences économique*, p. 59.

Given these external supports and the relatively sound condition of Belgian finances by the fall of 1926, it is not surprising that the stabilization was easily effected without internal deflation. In fact, capital began to flow to Belgium and the gold and exchange holdings of the National Bank, as well as the note circulation, continued to rise until 1933.[56] There is, then, some doubt as to whether the foreign loan was required, at least in the amount actually borrowed. Foreign capital had already begun to flow in immediately after the July debacle[57] and the flow continued through 1933.[58] On the other hand, the display of confidence on the part of private and central bankers may well have played a part in this return flow. Even though the flow began before the extension of the credit and loan was announced, it is by no means certain that it would have continued had the loan not been forthcoming.

The need for the credit seems to be an entirely different matter. The fact that the credit was never drawn upon is not, in itself, conclusive proof that it was unnecessary. The private bankers clearly insisted on a central bank credit as a condition for handling the loan, and it is possible that the loan was needed. But, in view of the internal situation in Belgium at the end of the summer of 1926, the demand of the bankers for central bank support seems scarcely justified. Nor can it be said that it was a means of using the prestige and power of the central bankers to impose conditions of restraint on the Belgian government or the National Bank of Belgium. No significant form of control was set up[59] as to the use of the proceeds of the loan and no specific revenues were pledged as security for the loan. Even in the issue over the management of the National Bank of Belgium, which had been a matter of earlier concern, Francqui would have provided the solution without any pressure from the other central bankers since he, too, did not have confidence in Hautain. There is every reason to believe that the bond issue would

---

[56] Shepherd, *The Monetary Experience of Belgium, 1914–1936*, p. 195. The gold and exchange reserves of the bank rose from about 5.5 billion francs in 1927 to 13.4 billion in 1933 and the note circulation from 9.6 billion in 1927 to 17.8 billion in 1933. There was a small drop in the gold and exchange reserves in 1931 as a result of losses on sterling holdings, but it was an insignificant drop.

[57] See p. 26.

[58] Baudhuin, *Histoire économique de la Belgique 1914–1939*, p. 168.

[59] The Bank of England did, however, request and receive regular, periodic progress reports from the National Bank of Belgium.

have been marketable without any significant further reduction of the issue price [60] even if it had not had the moral support of a central bank credit. One is inclined to suspect that the private bankers were led, in the course of the Janssen negotiations, to realize what support such a central bank credit could provide and to recognize that its extension could be arranged. A statement on the loan prospectus to the effect that a group of central banks were extending a credit in connection with this operation, with the implication that they were putting a seal of approval on the loan issue, would certainly add to the attractiveness of the bonds. In any case, the precedent of combining a central bank credit with a stabilization loan issue was now set and the practice would continue.

The attitude of the Bank of England and of the Federal Reserve Bank of New York toward this aspect of the credit extension is of some interest. The Federal Reserve Bank of New York always insisted on seeing the proof of the prospectus of a loan issue prior to publication, particularly from the point of view of passing on the wording of any reference to a central bank credit. By judicious choice of words, it attempted to avoid the implication that the central banks were passing on the quality of the loan issue itself, but it should be obvious that some such implication remains no matter how innocuously the prospectus is worded. The Bank of England, on the other hand, recognized that the mere extension of a central bank credit carried this implication whether intended or not.[61]

As far as the central bankers were concerned, the entire negotiations were handled by the Bank of England and the Federal Reserve Bank of New York. The other central banks were invited to participate after these two were satisfied with the program and on the basis of what sketchy, summary information these two chose to forward to

[60] Shepherd, for example, says: "It might be argued with fairness that 94 was too low an issue price for a 7 per cent loan in view of Francqui's reforms—but mysterious are the ways and persuasive the language of international bankers. They decided on 94. The 'spread' between the issue price and the net yield on Belgium, $4,000,000, seems large; but it was not exceptional, according to bankers' testimony before the Senate Finance Committee in December 1931" (Shepherd, *The Monetary Experience of Belgium, 1914–1936*, p. 167). In a footnote, he points out that Lamont of J. P. Morgan testified that the spread on international loans might be anywhere from 3 to 6 per cent.

[61] See pp. 110, 118, 121, and 126–27 for the attitudes adopted by the two banks in this connection in the Rumanian negotiations.

the others. In essence, they were asked to trust the judgment of Norman and Strong. This procedure was, no doubt, essential, since to have all potential participants take part in the negotiations would have been impossibly cumbersome. On the other hand, the other central banks would only be able to form a valid independent appraisal of the program if they had had the advantage of participation in the negotiations. The invitations to the other central banks were extended by the Bank of England since, until this time at least, it was the general practice of the Federal Reserve Bank of New York to deal with European central banks on such matters through the Bank of England. Norman realized that the other banks were being asked to accept his and Strong's judgment and accepted the moral responsibility that this entailed.[62] Certainly it was not possible for the Bank of England or the Federal Reserve Bank to accept legal responsibility for the safety of either the credit or the loan even if they had wished to do so, but a moral responsibility to the market and to the other central banks was hardly avoidable.

The order in which the invitations were extended was, at the very least, undiplomatic. To have delayed approaching the Bank of France until after at least tentative commitments had been received from nine other banks, including some of the smaller European central banks and one non-European one, was hardly calculated to flatter French sensibilities.[63] Perhaps even worse was the fact that the Bank of France was invited only after the Reichsbank had already joined the consortium. This aspect of the negotiations was treated somewhat more diplomatically in the Italian stabilization. Nevertheless, the Bank of France still complained of not being treated as an equal by the Bank of England.

[62] See pp. 84–85 for the attitude of the Federal Reserve authorities of the time on this point in the Polish negotiations.

[63] In February 1928, Moreau finally made a visit to the bank of England during which he complained of being slighted and demanded treatment on the basis of equality (Moreau, *Souvenirs*, pp. 505–506).

Cecil Lubbock, then Deputy Governor of the Bank of England, wrote to Strong that "Moreau thinks that hitherto we have been leaving him out in the cold: he claims from henceforth to be treated as an equal . . ." (letter, February 28, 1928, Lubbock to Strong, Strong Papers, Bank of England). It must be conceded, however, that Moreau was also pressing Rumanian stabilization at the time and this position was, to some extent, a gambit.

Chapter III. ITALY

Italian stabilization was not chronologically the next operation of this type,[1] but it was another case in which the Bank of England and the Federal Reserve Bank of New York cooperated in assuming the leadership of the central bank consortium. The Italian credit was arranged with remarkable ease. The entire operation, from the first approach of the Italians to legal stabilization, was completed within one month.

Italy, after Mussolini took over the government in October 1922, presented a monetary picture that was essentially different from that of most Continental nations. In the immediate postwar years, the Italian budget deficit was as large as that of any other ex-belligerent nation of the period, reaching 14.235 billion lire in the fiscal year 1920–1921. But as early as 1921–1922 this deficit had been cut in half and the budget position continued to improve until, in the fiscal year 1924–1925, there was a surplus of 417 million lire.[2] This budgetary improvement was, of course, reflected somewhat in the public debt figures. The internal debt reached its maximum figure of 95.544 billion lire on June 30, 1923. Thereafter it continued to fall, although slowly, until at the end of 1926 it stood at 84.485 billion lire, of which 21.28 billion represented floating debt.[3] During these earlier years, the improvements were apparently achieved without undue deflation. The unemployment figures fell steadily

[1] Poland stabilized *de jure* about two months earlier.

[2] Memorandum, November 30, 1926, "The Value of the Lira," Federal Reserve, Correspondence, Banca d'Italia.

[3] Count Volpi and Prof. Bonaldo Stringher, *The Financial Reconstruction of Italy* (New York, 1927), pp. 102–103.

during the period. The annual monthly maximum was 391,974 in January 1923 and fell each year thereafter until the annual monthly maximum in December 1926 was 181,493. The monthly minimums for the year also fell from 178,612 in August 1923 to 79,678 in July 1926.[4] Nevertheless, the exchange value of the lira, which had fallen to approximately one-fourth of its prewar value in the immediate postwar period, remained weak. The government intervened in an attempt to stabilize the lira in the vicinity of 4 United States cents in early 1925, but the attempt failed and the lira broke sharply.[5] This failure undoubtedly played some part in the replacement in July 1925 of Alberto de Stefani as Minister of Finance by Count Giuseppe Volpi di Misurata.

Volpi immediately instituted another attempt at stabilization. At this time, Italy had three banks of issue rather than one: the Bank of Italy, the Bank of Naples, and the Bank of Sicily. As a result, the stabilization operation, as well as monetary policy in general, was necessarily in the hands of the Treasury rather than of a central bank.[6] By September 1925 the lira had been pegged at about 4 United States cents and it was held at this level until April 1926.[7] The stabilization attempt was aided greatly by the announcement of war debt settlements with the United States and Britain, both of which were very favorable to Italy. The Italian-American debt settlement, which was reached on November 14, 1925, also served to open the American financial market to Italian borrowing.[8] Within less than a week of the settlement, J. P. Morgan and Company, financial agents of the Italian government in the United States, announced the flotation by a syndicate that it was heading of a $100-million Italian stabilization loan. The bonds, issued at 94.5, were heavily oversubscribed by banking and investment houses and

[4] François Perroux, *Contribution à l'étude de l'économie et des finances publiques de l'Italie depuis la guerre* (Paris, 1929), p. 309. But the figures rose sharply in 1927 to a maximum of 414,283 in December and a minimum of 214,603 in June.

[5] *Ibid.*, p. 272.

[6] The Treasury retained ultimate legal control over monetary policy even after the sole right of note issue was consolidated in the hands of the Bank of Italy.

[7] William Adams Brown, Jr., *The International Gold Standard Reinterpreted 1914–1934* (New York, 1940), p. 428.

[8] See fn. 10, p. 18.

yielded the Italian government approximately $90 million.[9] The lira was held at about four United States cents until late April 1926, when speculative pressure developed against it and the defense was abandoned.[10] By the end of the summer, the lira had fallen below 3.3 cents. The Italian Treasury, however, had wisely abandoned support before committing the bulk of the proceeds of the Morgan loan to the effort so that these resources were still available for a new try.

Volpi now began to prepare a more careful and comprehensive program. The first measure was taken by Royal Decree published May 22, 1926 (confirmed by law on June 25, 1926). Effective July 1, 1926, this step consolidated the right of note issue in the Bank of Italy. The Bank of Naples and the Bank of Sicily transferred the gold and equivalent assets which they held as cover against their note issues to the Bank of Italy, and the Bank of Italy assumed the responsibility of replacing their outstanding notes with its own. Prior to the transfer, the Italian Treasury was to repay advances in the amount of 125 million lire, which had been made by the two southern banks, and the note circulation would be reduced by this amount.[11] Beyond some slight increase in the reserve ratio against the outstanding note issue of the Bank of Italy, the principal effect of the measure was to make possible the transfer of responsibility for monetary policy from the Treasury to a central bank, i.e., to the Bank of Italy. While some such steps were later effected in practice, the Treasury continued to hold the legal reins with respect to monetary policy. Formally, the bank was still unable even to change the

---

[9] The loan absorbed a prior credit of $50 million, which the Morgan group had extended to the Italian government (Shepherd, *The Monetary Experience of Belgium, 1914–1936*, pp. 125–26). See also fn. 25, p. 23.

[10] In a cable of May 17, 1926, to T. W. Lamont of J. P. Morgan & Co., Volpi indicated that the defense of the lira had cost the Italian Treasury little and attributed the speculation to general confusion in the Continental exchanges at the time of the British coal strike (cable, May 17, 1926, Giovanni Fummi to T. W. Lamont [Volpi sent the cable through Fummi, who was Morgan's representative in Italy], Federal Reserve, Correspondence, Italy, Banca d'Italia, 1926). Certainly, the French and Belgian francs shared in this pressure in the spring of 1926 and it is not clear to what extent this movement was a consequence of the general sympathetic movement of the Belgian and Italian currencies with the French franc. But it is difficult to see how this weakness of the Continental exchanges could be a consequence of the British strike, which should have had the opposite effect.

[11] Stringher, "Unification of Bank-Note Issue and Currency Deflation," in Volpi and Stringher, *The Financial Reconstruction of Italy*, pp. 56–59.

rediscount rate without Treasury approval. A second significant measure taken at this time was the appointment of a special committee of experts to study the problem of stabilization.

About this time, Strong paid his first visit to Governor Stringher of the Bank of Italy and, despite some reservations with respect to his own authority to deal with foreign governments, Strong agreed to an informal meeting with Volpi and Stringher held on May 26, 1926. The meeting was, of course, concerned with an Italian stabilization program and Strong provided a number of general suggestions with respect to such a program.[12] He stressed the need for a careful study of the Italian wage and price structure in relation to world prices in order that a value for the lira might be selected which would require neither excessive deflation nor inflation. In this connection, he pointed out that "no currency inflation having occurred for some time and the value of the lira having been fairly steady for over a year, internal prices and wages may have largely, if not wholly, readjusted to present world prices and conditions, but as to this, further study is desirable." [13]

He also stressed the importance of freeing the central bank from political control and putting the execution of a stabilization program in the hands of the bank. If feasible, he recommended that the bank have a portfolio of government securities available for use in controlling the money market. He suggested the desirability of simultaneous action with Belgium and France, but recognized that this might not be possible. In a later memorandum which he anticipated would be shown to Volpi, he put the point rather vaguely as follows: "Experience seems to indicate a certain interdependence between currencies of different countries, the effects of depreciation in one country being reflected in another country, doubtless because of the effect of changing costs of production upon international markets for goods. While collaboration with other countries may not be possible, concurrent action would of course be helpful." [14] But he pointed out that, if cooperation with France were not possible, the foreign exchange resources of Italy would probably have to be larger

[12] Letter, May 26, 1926, Strong to Harrison, Strong Papers, European Trips; and memorandum, June 8, 1926, enclosed with letter, June 9, 1926, Strong to Harrison, Federal Reserve, Correspondence, Italy, Banca d'Italia, 1926.
[13] Memorandum, June 8, 1926, *ibid.*   [14] *Ibid.*

than would have been necessary had the franc been successfully stabilized. If foreign credits were required, he recommended that they
be arranged in a number of countries so as to provide a broad background of responsibility and confidence.

Following a speech by Mussolini at Pesaro on August 17, 1926, in
which he promised a strong defense of the lira, deflationary measures began to be instituted. At the end of August, the Bank of Italy
was instructed to conduct its credit transactions so that the total of
such transactions at the end of September should, under no circumstances, exceed the corresponding total at the end of August.[15] Already, Strong began to anticipate an approach from the Italians. On
September 4, 1926, he wrote Harrison from Paris:

> Pursuing the methods characteristic of Mussolini and Volpi, and follow-
> ing our conversations in Rome last May, they went on ahead with the ap-
> pointment of a committee and the development of a program without any
> publicity, until finally on the 31st of August they published decrees for
> the adoption of certain important preliminary steps, which, I notice, have
> been fully published and much commented upon in the American
> newspapers . . .
> About a week before, there had been some unusual developments in the
> lira exchange in London, where the spread between spot and forward got
> up to 75% per annum. It looked to me as though they were getting ready
> to give the lira a boost and then announce something, and I told Dwight
> Morrow and Dean Jay that it would surprise me if we did not hear some-
> thing from them in a few days.[16]

A Royal Decree of September 7, 1926, introduced the first major
steps. The entire proceeds of the 1925 Morgan loan were turned
over to the Bank of Italy and the Treasury debt to the bank was reduced by 2.5 billion lire as a counter-entry. In addition, the government announced its intention of paying off the balance of this debt
to the bank by means of minimum annual appropriations in the
budget of 500 million lire. The decree set a limit on the total note
circulation which the bank could issue for ordinary commercial requirements. The ceiling applied to only certain limited types of

[15] Stringher in Volpi and Stringher, *The Financial Reconstruction of Italy*,
p. 74.
[16] Letter, September 4, 1926, Strong to Harrison, Federal Reserve, Correspondence, Italy, Banca d'Italia, 1926.

transactions, however, so that it covered only about one-third of the outstanding note issue of the bank, Finally, the decree provided for the withdrawal from circulation or conversion into silver coin of outstanding Treasury notes in denominations of 25 lire or less.[17]

These latter provisions of the decree had, of course, little practical meaning, but the overall psychological effect was significant particularly concerning the fear of conversion of the entire floating debt. As a result, there was a heavy excess demand from the Italian public for reimbursement of Treasury bills. Rumors of a forced conversion and the fact that several series of multi-year bonds were maturing in the near future fed this demand for redemption of bills.[18] By decree of November 6, 1926, the government did in fact order a forced conversion operation known as the Lictor Loan. Conversion was mandatory for all securities with a maturity of seven years or less and optional for longer maturities up to nine years. Although the effect of the operation was to raise the total public debt somewhat, it virtually eliminated the floating debt [19] except for slightly over 4 billion lire of notes issued by the Bank of Italy for account of the state.

In view of these developments in the Italian situation, both the Bank of England and the Federal Reserve Bank of New York were giving some consideration, in November of 1926, to their likely reaction to a request for assistance from the Bank of Italy should such a request be forthcoming. Norman did not feel that the time was as yet ripe for stabilization. Clay feels that his principal reservation was the lack of independence of the Bank of Italy [20] and this factor certainly played a large part in determining his attitude. But he also had some doubts about Italian political stability and about the adequacy of the preliminary preparations. In a letter to Harrison of July 27, 1928, Strong reported on some discussions he had had with H. A. Siepmann of the Bank of England and wrote: "He said that Governor Norman, about a year before the December [1927] meet-

[17] Stringher, in Volpi and Stringher, *The Financial Reconstruction of Italy*, pp. 64–67.
[18] Perroux, *Contribution*, pp. 252–53; see also, Brown, *The International Gold Standard*, p. 429.
[19] Perroux, *Contribution*, pp. 255–58.
[20] Sir Henry Clay, *Lord Norman* (London, 1957), pp. 257–58.

ings in London, had been definitely opposed to doing anything in
Italy, because of complete lack of confidence in the Mussolini regime. He thought it needed a longer period of test and that much
more had to be accomplished in a preliminary way to prepare for
stabilization, before stabilization could be effected." [21]

Some of the same doubts were present at the Federal Reserve
Bank as well, although it is quite possible that the Reserve might
have been willing to set them aside had the Bank of Italy requested
aid. On November 16, 1926, Robert Warren of the New York Bank
prepared a memorandum for Harrison on the progress of Italian stabilization in which he concluded:

> The measures taken by the Italian government form so far a comprehen-
> sive, coordinated program, evidently to be capped by definitive stabiliza-
> tion and some sort of foreign credits or loans. They give promise of success,
> except under two contingencies.
>   1. There may be an attempt to fix the lira at too high a value. Any value
>   over four cents will be difficult to maintain; but an effort at
>   some such figure as a ratio of one to five (say 3.70 cents) should be
>   possible of maintenance without too great sacrifice. A 4 to 1 ratio
>   would probably collapse.
>   2. A political upset would probably have serious consequences. Such an
>   upset becomes more likely if the lira is forced too high, as it is
>   questionable if the Mussolini government could survive a period
>   of "hard times."
> While the actual measures taken have been good, they have been rather
> clumsily applied, with an apparent effort toward sensational surprises
> rather than a steady upbuilding of confidence. To some extent this was nec-
> essary because of the decline of the lira in the summer at least partly in
> sympathy with the French franc.
> The bank is not legally more independent than it has been. On the
> other hand, with government finances in good shape, there is little incen-
> tive for the government to abuse its legal power over the bank. The fact
> remains, however, that while the present government may not abuse the
> bank, its successor may. There is little assurance of continuity of the pres-
> ent sound program.
> While Italy is just about ready for the final plunge, I do not think the
> Federal Reserve Bank could entertain a proposal to grant a credit except
> under two [sic] conditions:

[21] Letter, July 27, 1928, Strong to Harrison, Strong Papers, European Trips,
1928.

1. That the new value of the lira be determined by reference to economic facts, and not by national pride or the whim of speculators. An attempt to peg the lira at a fancy price, even though it might prove successful, is too hazardous to be encouraged by the Federal Reserve Reserve Bank of New York.
2. That any fundamental change in Italian monetary policy during the proposed life of the credit will be considered as creating a new situation and necessitate a review of the proposition.
3. That continuity of the program be assured for the life of the credit by granting Bank of Italy adequate power to assume responsibility for the currency.[22]

By November 30, 1926, however, Warren's view of the rate of stabilization had already undergone a subtle change. In a memorandum of that date on the value of the lira, he concludes by saying:

Economically, it was probably a mistake to let the lire [*sic*] rise above 3¾ cents; but it is a condition, not a theory that confronts us. Given $100,000,000 and capable bank management, the maintenance of the lire at 4¼ cents does not seem impossible.

It does look difficult. It probably means deflation, hard times, strikes, discontent by workmen who see their wages and their jobs threatened, industrialists who lose their markets, and farmers who find the prices of their crops going down just at harvest. Against these materialistic disadvantages may be set the profits of speculators and the patriotic joy of thinking that one's currency has been stabilized at 23% instead of 20% of its nominal value.

Still, compared to what other countries have undergone, the amount of hardship likely to be imposed on the people of Italy by setting the lira at 4¼ is far from excessive. It need not cause great concern except for the unstable character of the Italian government.[23]

However, the Bank of Italy did not ask for any assistance at this time. In fact, Italy did not yet attempt even *de facto* stabilization. Instead, in February 1927 the National Institute of Foreign Exchange, which had been a separate Treasury agency, was reorganized to become essentially a department of the Bank of Italy. The bank, through the institute, then carried through the government's policy

[22] Memorandum, November 16, 1926, subject: "Progress of Italian Stabilization," Warren to Harrison, Federal Reserve, Correspondence, Italy, Banca d'Italia, 1926.
[23] Memorandum, "The Value of the Lira," November 30, 1926, *ibid.*

of distinct exchange appreciation by means of intervention in the market. By June 1927 the lira had risen to 5.5819 United States cents, a level slightly higher than that ultimately adopted for legal stabilization.[24] The effort resulted in depression and unemployment, but the rate was achieved and maintained. There then followed a period of *de facto* stabilization.

By early November 1927 both Norman and Strong had come to the conclusion that Italian *de jure* stabilization was imminent. Strong wrote Norman on November 9:

Quite confidentially, I am willing to risk the opinion that Italy is rapidly approaching the point where stabilization will be desired and probably may be accomplished with security. When the time arrives to face the question I should like very much to feel that you and I are in accord as to the wisdom of their undertaking de jure stabilization, and after all necessary investigation, that we may be in accord in aiding them to do so.[25]

By letter dated November 22, 1927, Norman expressed agreement with Strong's analysis and with the desirability of the two banks cooperating to provide assistance. But events were already moving rapidly. The same day that Norman's letter was written, Luigi Podesta, the New York representative of the Italian Exchange Institute, called on Strong and advised him that Stringher had just sent a confidential message to Podesta asking if Governor Strong could refer him to some person in London with whom Stringher could converse "with understanding on very important matters." Strong suggested that any communication could be transmitted to him through Governor Norman or, if that were not feasible, probably through Mr. Walter Whigham of Morgan, Grenfell and Company.

Stringher replied through Podesta that, since the purpose of his London visit was to confer with the Governor of the Bank of England, he felt it would be best to have Mr. Whigham represent Governor Strong. Harrison immediately pointed out that the bank could not designate anyone then in London to represent them, but that Whigham could only serve as an intermediary for the transmis-

24 Brown, *The International Gold Standard*, pp. 430–31.
25 Letter, November 9, 1927, Strong to Norman, Strong Papers, Bank of England.

sion of messages.[26] Stringher's initial contact, consequently, was only with the Bank of England. Immediately after that contact, Cecil Lubbock, Deputy Governor of the Bank of England, telephoned to Strong on November 29, 1927. He said that Norman had received satisfactory assurances from Stringher as to his desire to cooperate with the banks of issue, the size of the gold holdings of the Bank of Italy, and its ability to put through a program. Stringher had indicated that the Bank of Italy did not propose a long-term loan, but desired a one-year credit of $100,000,000 from the Federal Reserve and the Bank of England. Norman had emphasized that precedent, and a continued desire for cooperation, would probably make it necessary for the credit to be with many banks of issue rather than just two. Stringher had not considered this type of credit and asked time to think it over. The vital questions of the rate of stabilization; what, if anything, would be asked in the way of private credits; or the imminence of stabilization had, however, not yet been discussed.[27] On the same day, Norman also cabled New York that Stringher had asked for Strong or a representative of Strong's to come to London to take part in negotiations for a central bank credit.[28]

Even before Strong sailed for London on December 2, there was a cable exchange between Norman and Strong over the question of whether and how Moreau should be advised of the pending negotiations in view of the political difficulties between France and Italy over conflicting interests in Eastern Europe. Italy's conclusion of a pact of friendship with Hungary in 1927 had represented an important threat to French anti-revisionist policy in Eastern Europe. In addition, the signing of a Franco-Yugoslav treaty in November 1927 as a counter to the Italo-Albanian pact of a year earlier had aroused Italian fury and resulted in the conclusion in late November 1927 of a formal military pact between Italy and Albania.[29] As a conse-

[26] All of the information on the Podesta contact is taken from Harrison's memorandum to the confidential files, November 25, 1927, Federal Reserve, Correspondence, Banca d'Italia, 1926.

[27] Memorandum, November 29, 1927, subject: "Bank of Italy," Harrison to Strong, Strong Papers, Harrison to Strong, 1926–27.

[28] Cable, November 29, 1927, Norman to Strong, Federal Reserve, Correspondence, Italy, Banca d'Italia, 1926.

[29] Seton-Watson, *Eastern Europe between the Wars 1918–1941*, pp. 371–74.

quence of these maneuverings for alliances in Eastern Europe, Franco-Italian relations were at this very moment extremely strained. Nevertheless, Strong urged that some sort of arrangements be made with Stringher as soon as possible so that somehow Moreau would be advised, since he felt that it was extremely important to have France participate in any credit arrangement.[30] The agreement in principle of the Bank of France was, in fact, received on December 4, 1927. On that date, Siepmann visited Moreau and Rist in Paris and asked whether Moreau would trust Norman and Strong to examine under what conditions a credit of $100 million (£20 million) to the Bank of Italy for stabilization purposes would be possible and whether Moreau would accept the division: £5 million Federal Reserve, £3 million each Banks of England, France, and Germany, and £1 million each Banks of Belgium, Holland, and Switzerland. Moreau expressed complete agreement.[31]

The Norman-Strong-Stringher negotiations opened on December 13, 1927, and from the beginning the only serious question seems to have concerned the rate selected for stabilization. The market rate for the lira was then, and had been for some time, about 90 lire to the pound sterling and the proposed stabilization rate was 92.5 to the pound, or 5.263 United States cents. Both Norman and Strong felt that this rate was much too high for safety but, on the other hand, they felt that stabilization should be at the prevailing market rate. Hence, if the selected rate was to be somewhat lower, stabilization must be deferred in order to permit time for the market to adjust in an orderly fashion. In the final analysis, however, they both preferred that the Italians assume the responsibility involved rather than that they assume it by insisting on a different rate. Consequently, within a few days they accepted Stringher's assurances that the rate was justified and safe.[32] By December 16, 1927, agreement had also been reached to limit the central bank credit to $75 million and to seek a private bank credit to the Bank of Italy for $50 million.[33] Harrison had some doubts on this score since all previous

[30] Cable exchange, December 1, 1927, Norman and Strong, Federal Reserve, Correspondence, Italy, Banca d'Italia, 1926.

[31] Moreau, *Souvenirs*, pp. 440–41.

[32] Cable, December 16, 1927, Strong to Harrison, Federal Reserve, Correspondence, Italy, Banca d'Italia, 1926.

[33] *Ibid.*

private loans and credits had been to governments, and he felt that it was essential to keep the private and central bank assistance separate in the mind of the public.[34] Extending the private credit to the Bank of Italy would, he felt, tend to confuse the two credits. This solution of a private credit to the Bank of Italy was adopted, however, in order to avoid any discrediting of the 1925 Italian stabilization loan by an indication that the government needed further assistance.

The central bank credit was agreed upon on December 20, 1927.[35] This time, the Federal Reserve, including the Board, accepted without question a commission charge of 0.5 per cent and a minimum interest rate of 6 per cent against amounts drawn. At the same time that the central bank credit was extended, J. P. Morgan and Company extended a credit of $25 million and Morgan Grenfell and Company, Baring Brothers and Company, Ltd., Hambros Bank, Ltd., and N. M. Rothschild and Sons jointly extended one of £5 million to the Bank of Italy.[36] The stabilization decree was published in Rome on December 22, 1927.

The doubts which Norman and Strong felt with respect to the chosen rate of stabilization were shared by other central bankers as well. Strong reported that, during a conversation in the summer of 1928, Schacht had told him:

[34] Harrison memorandum to the confidential files, December 21, 1927, subject: "Bank of Italy," Harrison Collection, Binder 45.
[35] Federal Reserve, Correspondence, Banca d'Italia. Participation was as follows:

Austria	$2,500,000
Belgium	$5,000,000
Czechoslovakia	£400,000
Denmark	$500,000
Egypt	£100,000
Finland	$1,500,000
France	£2,000,000
Germany	£2,000,000
Great Britain	£2,000,000
Hungary	£1,000,000
Japan	£500,000
Netherlands	Fls. 12,000,000
Poland	£500,000
Sweden	Kr. 7,500,000
Switzerland	Sw. Fr. 10,000,000
United States	$15,000,000

[36] Federal Reserve, Correspondence, Italy, Banca d'Italia, 1926.

He liked the Italian plan in all respects except the rate of stabilization and attributed this, not to any oversight on our part, but to the fact that Volpi was entirely responsible so far as he controlled matters in permitting the lira to reach such a high level prior to stabilization being effective. He says in his opinion it is impossible to stabilize in such a case as Italy except at substantially the market rate at the time, and he was delighted when I recounted what had transpired at London and told him that the record showed that we had questioned the rate very seriously but had taken the position that the responsibility rested upon Italy, and the real question was whether they should stabilize at the present rate or defer stabilization for a period long enough to bring about a reduction of the rate without too sharp a readjustment of prices, wages, etc. But, of course, they had their orders from Mussolini and had to go ahead anyway; but I think our record is perfectly clear. Schacht anticipates a period of difficulty in Italy because of the high value placed upon the lira.[37]

Governor Franck of the National Bank of Belgium expressed similar views.[38] Experience demonstrated that these doubts were, to a considerable extent, justified and it is difficult to understand why the central bankers insisted that *de jure* stabilization could not be combined with devaluation with respect to the prevailing market rate. While the stabilization was maintained up to the time of British suspension, it was only at the price of heavy deflationary pressure. Even so, the lira had fallen below par by the summer of 1928 and remained at a low level. On the other hand, Italy had been suffering from deflationary pressures even before *de jure* stabilization and it is unlikely that a lower parity for the lira would have set off serious inflation. Two questions then arise. Why did the Italians insist on this rate? Why did all the central bankers permit their doubts on this point to be set aside?

One of the reasons that has been advanced for the insistence by the Italians on this particular rate has to do with Treasury finances.[39] Writing up the gold and equivalent assets of the Bank of Italy to this new value resulted in a paper profit that was just sufficient to wipe out the debt of the state to the bank. This explanation is adequate to justify why the rate was not set even higher, but it hardly explains resistance to a lower level. It might be considered

[37] Letter, July 12, 1928, Strong to Harrison, Strong Papers, European Trips, 1928.
[38] Letter, July 20, 1928, *ibid.*   [39] Perroux, *Contribution*, p. 294.

that the Italians were reluctant to defer legal stabilization while the market rate moved to a lower level. But the market rate had scarcely been market determined, nor had the Italians shown any great urgency up to this moment about taking the final step. In any case, it is not clear why such market adjustment had to precede legal stabilization. It appears in fact that, within the limitation of the financial constraint mentioned above, the Italians were indeed motivated by considerations of national prestige, coupled perhaps with a desire to hold the cost of imports to as low a level as possible.

The second question is the more interesting in the context of this study. Part of the reason for the central bankers' acceptance of the Italian decision was, of course, a reluctance to accept the responsibility of putting a moral seal of approval on the rate chosen, particularly when the central bankers insisted upon the extension of private bank credits at the same time. It would appear that the central bankers could have objected to the chosen rate without necessarily having forced any particular alternative on Italy. Such a stand would seem to have been preferable to the acceptance of a rate that they clearly felt might endanger the private credit and any other capital that might now be attracted to Italy. In addition, there were other issues, such as the independence of the Bank of Italy, which could have been substituted as a reason not to extend a credit. But the independence of the Bank of Italy was not made a vital issue either. It would appear that there was simply a reluctance to refuse a request for assistance from another central bank regardless of the reason for the refusal. The stipulation of any conditions to which the borrower seriously objected was beginning to be viewed as an indication of unwillingness to cooperate. The Bank of England and the Federal Reserve Bank of New York did not want to take upon themselves the responsibility of a refusal and be accused of such unwillingness to cooperate to aid a central bank in difficulty. The other banks were in an even poorer position to raise any serious question. They had not had the advantage of participation in the negotiations and had, in fact, agreed to accept the judgment of the Bank of England and the Federal Reserve Bank. The number of participants indicates that the inclination was to participate in any case simply as an indication of the individual bank's desire to cooperate with the others. The invitations were, in fact, couched in such terms as to make any refusal a virtual admission of lack of belief in the principle of cooperation. The credit extension itself, rather than genuine assistance to the stabilizing nation, appears to have become the end sought.

This element was also reflected in the failure to insist upon real independence for the Bank of Italy. By their own announced principles, this was an essential condition for effective prosecution of a stabilization program. Having violated it in this case, it became very difficult to insist upon even more stringent control measures for other nations. It was true that the need for controls might vary from country to country; but it was hardly consistent to argue, after having made this concession to Italy, that the control of an adviser over a legally independent Rumanian National Bank, however weak his control, was inadequate.

As in the case of the Belgian credit, the entire negotiations were handled by the Bank of England and the Federal Reserve Bank of New York. Again, the other central banks were invited to participate on the basis of trust in the judgment of Norman and Strong. Lester Chandler feels that this, plus the fact that Norman had not insisted that Italy go through the Financial Committee of the League, injured Moreau's feelings.[40] Certainly, Moreau did complain a few months later that the Bank of France was not being treated as an equal, although there is considerable suspicion that the complaint was really a convenient support for his espousal of Rumanian stabilization. In many respects, there was less cause for complaint in this case than there had been when Belgium stabilized. The Bank of France was advised at an early stage in the negotiations on the same basis as were the other banks of issue, apart from the two leaders. Surely it was impossible to conduct effective negotiations with sixteen banks represented on an equal basis. If the leadership were to be enlarged by one or two, on what basis should the selection be made? By late 1927 the Bank of France had acquired great power in the international money markets. On the other hand, France had not yet legally stabilized so that the contribution of the Bank of France to the credit could not even be in her

40 Chandler, *Benjamin Strong, Central Banker,* pp. 389–90.

own currency, but had to be in sterling. On this basis, several of the other banks—not least among them, the Reichsbank—had stronger reasons to claim a right to participate in the negotiations. If the protestations of the Bank of France were genuine, it appears that it was demanding the best of two worlds: the prestige and power of a major bank of issue along with the freedom of action which an un-stabilized exchange permitted.

Chapter IV. POLAND

Despite the reservations of the central bankers with regard to the rate chosen for Italian stabilization, the ease with which credit assistance for the Italian effort was arranged stands in striking contrast to the difficulties encountered in arranging such assistance for Poland. In some respects this is a little surprising, in others it is easily understood. The preparatory measures for both Belgian and Italian stabilization were a series of rather pragmatic steps taken by the Belgian and Italian governments without international consultation. The stabilization programs, to the extent that they can be considered as such, resulted from these preliminary actions rather than having been carefully thought out programs prepared in advance of the stabilization efforts. The final Polish effort, on the other hand, was based upon a comprehensive plan prepared by a foreign advisory commission. From this point of view, one might have expected the credit negotiations in the Polish instance to have been more straightforward than those of the other two.

While both Belgium and Italy experienced serious postwar inflation, however, in neither case did it reach the catastrophic proportions of the Polish experience. In this respect, only German and Austrian experience was comparable to that of Poland, and even Austrian postwar note issue did not expand to the same extent as Polish.[1] In addition, Polish political stability was much more precarious than that of either Belgium or Italy. Certainly Belgium experienced changes of government that were not always easily effected, but the danger of revolutionary change was relatively remote. The Fascist government in Italy, while it may have been shocking to the

[1] Pierre Robin, *La Réforme monétaire en Pologne* (Paris, 1932), p. 13.

liberal elements in other countries, was so well established by 1927 that there was little danger of its overthrow unless it created the necessary conditions itself. Poland, on the other hand, was constantly faced with the danger of violent political change, which finally took place with the Pilsudski coup of 1926. Finally, the political interests of other nations were not so deeply involved in Belgium and Italy as they were in Poland. This is not to say that there were no political differences involving Belgium or Italy, but simply that they were not so fundamental or vital as those directly involving Eastern Europe, hence Poland. Thus, there were factors that placed Polish stabilization in a somewhat different category from Belgian or Italian, requiring somewhat different treatment and providing scope for major differences in the points of view of the various central banks.

In evaluating Polish monetary experience and understanding why there were some doubts about her capability to handle her own affairs without external guidance, it is important to realize the essential uniqueness of her postwar position. Poland was a new nation—more accurately, a nation reconstituted after more than a century of partition. In economic orientation, in the layout of her communications system, in administrative practice, and in monetary systems, she was a composite of isolated elements. Part of her territory had belonged to the Austrian Empire, part of it had been tied to Russia, and part of it to Germany. Almost the only unifying element was a sense of national identity. While she was not without trained public servants, they had been trained in widely disparate administrative systems. For the most part, they had been civil servants in an essentially Austrian, or German, or Russian hierarchy. Few, if any, had experience in positions of top-level responsibility. There was then a need, not only to organize a new government, but to weld together an entire new administrative machinery to carry on the mundane details of government. At the same time, there was an urgent need to tie the various parts of the territory together and to change economic orientations so as to create a nation in an economic as well as a political sense. Unlike other nations emerging from the war, therefore, Poland's task was not limited to one of reconstruction and, perhaps, a need to absorb some newly acquired territory. Superimposed on the extensive reconstruction requirements left from the war was

Poland's need to construct a new nation where none had existed before.

To further complicate this already tremendous task, the war did not end for Poland in 1918. For more than two additional years, Poland continued in a state of war. Nor was the burden of this war limited to the maintenance and supply of armies fighting on the frontiers. It reached its culminating point with the Bolshevik invasion in the summer of 1920 and continued, after the victorious defense of Warsaw, until early 1921.[2] Apart from the added physical destruction which this anti-Bolshevik war contributed to Poland's reconstruction burden, it meant that Poland necessarily began her reconstruction effort at least two years later than most other ex-belligerent countries. In addition, the extended war period added to the inflationary pressures, which would have been severe in any case.[3]

Finally, it should be remembered that Poland, in the early 1920s even more than today, was in the position of what in modern terminology would be referred to as a developing nation. About 65 per cent of her people were engaged in agriculture.[4] On the other hand, certain of her western and southern areas were already industrialized and provided a catalyst for stimulating further industrialization. Thus quite apart from the needs of reconstruction and rehabilitation, there was a heavy demand for imports of capital goods and a consequent expectation that there should be a deficit in the balance of payments on current account. If this deficit could not be balanced by capital imports, there was certain to be pressure on the exchange value of the Polish currency. Excessive inflation, which must add to foreign mistrust of the currency, would only increase the difficulty of supplying these postwar needs that could not possibly be supplied domestically. Heilperin points out that this is, in

[2] Michel Angelo Heilperin, *Le Problème monétaire d'après-guerre et sa solution en Pologne, en Autriche et en Tchécoslovaquie* (Paris, 1931), p. 66.

[3] Polish monetary circulation rose from 1 billion Polish marks in the last quarter of 1918 to 74 billion in the first quarter of 1921 (Bernard Blumenstrauch, *Le Nouveau régime monétaire en Pologne et son Rôle dans l'économie nationale* [Nancy, 1932], p. 24).

[4] "The Republic of Poland, its status at the close of 1926," prepared by the Foreign Information Service, Bankers Trust Company, p. 21 (Federal Reserve, Correspondence, Bank of Poland Credit).

fact, what happened. While there was internal depreciation of the Polish mark in the years 1921 to early 1924, it was less than the external depreciation. The result was that it became extremely expensive for Poland to purchase abroad and she became a good market for foreign buyers so that Poland ran a surplus on commercial balance in 1923.[5]

In view of these factors, it was to be expected that the Polish government, after hostilities finally ceased, would continue to resort to inflation as a means of satisfying its financial requirements. The practice was made even easier than it otherwise might have been by the fact that the bank of issue was a state bank inherited from the German administration. Monetary unification took place in 1920, when the Polish mark was introduced to replace the German marks. Russian rubles, and Austrian crowns then in circulation. In the middle of that year the Polish mark became the only legal tender currency. By 1923, however, it had long since ceased to be used as a standard of value and had largely been replaced by foreign currencies, notably United States dollars, as a medium of exchange.[6] In December of 1923 Ladislas Grabski took over as Finance Minister and head of the Polish government and initiated an attempt to bring a halt to the wild inflation. At this time, the mark had depreciated to the extent that one United States dollar exchanged for 6,375,000 Polish marks on the Warsaw Exchange.[7]

Already in the previous summer, a law had been passed establishing the prewar gold franc (value 19.3 United States cents) as a standard of value, although the mark remained the medium of exchange. Another law passed that summer authorized a capital levy, payable in foreign exchange or in Polish marks at the current market rate for the gold franc, designed to yield one billion gold francs.[8] No serious attempt was made to apply the law, however, until Grabski's government was granted *plein pouvoir* in January 1924 for a period of six months for the purpose of effecting monetary reform. Grabski had first tried to raise funds through a foreign

[5] Heilperin, *Le Problème monétaire*, p. 96.
[6] Robin, *La Réforme monétaire*, pp. 17–19, see also Thadée Mincer, *Le Zloty Polonais* (Paris, undated), p. 10.
[7] Mincer, *Le Zloty Polonais*, p. 12.
[8] *Ibid.*, p. 21, and Robin, *La Réforme monétaire*, p. 20.

loan but was refused by J. P. Morgan on the grounds of budget instability [9] and he could only raise a moderate loan of 400 million lire through the Banca Commerciale Italiana.[10] He therefore turned to the capital levy as a means of raising exceptional revenue. In addition, he instituted progressive income taxes, a system of monthly budgets, and halted further note issues by the state bank for account of the state.[11] By decree of February 7, 1924, he set the value of the gold franc at 1.8 million marks and charged the state bank with defending and maintaining this rate.[12]

At the same time, measures were instituted to organize a new bank of issue, the Bank of Poland. It was originally anticipated that 60 per cent of the bank's capital would be raised by private subscription and 40 per cent from the state Treasury. Public subscriptions were opened on January 25, 1924, and by March 31 private subscription had provided all but 1 per cent of the authorized capital.[13] The bank opened its doors on April 27, 1924, and replaced the state bank as the bank of issue. A few days later the new currency unit, the zloty, was introduced into circulation. Its value was fixed at that of the gold franc, or at 5.18 zlotys to the United States dollar.[14]

Even before these measures had had a chance to take effect, the consequence of their announcement was a return of confidence in the Polish currency. *De facto* stabilization was already achieved in January 1924 and gold and foreign exchange began to flow into the state bank. With the return of confidence, there was a reduction in the hoarding and use of foreign currency, which began to be turned into the bank. In addition, there was a marked decrease in the velocity of circulation as people began again to hold Polish currency. As a result, there was a need for an increase in the stock of money, which did expand in the spring of 1924.[15] Under the circumstances, however, this monetary expansion was not at all inflationary. In fact, the newly attained stability was maintained for well over a year.

[9] Robin *La Réforme monétaire*, p. 19.
[10] Blumenstrauch, *Le Nouveau régime*, p. 30.
[11] Robin, *La Réforme monétaire*, pp. 22–23.   [12] *Ibid.*, pp. 24–25.
[13] Mincer, *Le Zloty Polonais*, pp. 41–42.
[14] Blumenstrauch, *Le Nouveau régime*, p. 32.
[15] Heilperin, *Le Problème monétaire*, pp. 125–27.

But the seeds of a new inflation were built into Grabski's program. The capital levy failed to provide anything like the sums anticipated. It had been expected to bring in 333 million zlotys in the year 1924, but the actual receipts were only 199 million and these were collected with great difficulty.[16] The basic problem was that the payments called for far exceeded what could be reasonably paid out of revenues. They could only be met if the capitalist could realize at least some portion of his assets, and it was obviously impossible for all capitalists to do this simultaneously. To add to the difficulties, the harvest of 1924 was very poor and this added to the strain on the balance of payments. The government, faced with insufficient budgetary receipts, turned again to the issue of paper money. The issues were effected, not through expansion of the note issue of the Bank of Poland, but by the issue of subsidiary notes and coin by the Treasury. From early 1924 onward, the note issue of the Bank of Poland remained essentially constant in the neighborhood of 550 million zlotys and even fell off to 462 million by the end of July 1925. On the other hand, the issue of subsidiary notes and coin rose from 29 million zlotys on May 31, 1924, to 285 million on July 31, 1925.[17]

The government contracted a loan of $50 million with Dillon, Read and Company, then the financial agents of the Polish government in the United States. The first portion was floated in March of 1925, but only the nominal amount of $35 million could be placed at that time.[18] The final element which, added to the already deteriorated situation, brought on the break in the zloty was the open outbreak of a customs war with Germany in June 1925. Germany denounced her trade treaty with Poland, and German merchants began withdrawing the credits they had granted Polish importers.[19] The break came at the end of July when there was a sudden fall of about 10 per cent in the zloty exchange. On the request of Feliks Mlynarski, Vice President of the Bank of Poland, the Federal Reserve Bank of New York extended a $10-million credit to the Polish Bank. It was secured by a gold deposit at the Bank of England. The

[16] Robin, *La Réforme monétaire*, pp. 34–35.
[17] Heilperin, *Le Problème monétaire*, p. 130.
[18] Mincer, *Le Zloty Polonais*, p. 123, and Robin, *La Réforme monétaire*, p. 41.
[19] Heilperin, *Le Problème monétaire*, p. 149.

credit was fully utilized in a vain attempt to prevent a depreciation of the zloty in the exchange market.[20] It was insufficient, however, to halt the fall of the zloty and support was withdrawn on August 27, 1925. The zloty continued downward until, in December 1925, it was at about 11 zlotys to the dollar.

Despite its failure, the Grabski attempt left Poland in greatly improved monetary condition. A new currency had been introduced and, while it too had now begun to depreciate, it still remained solid enough at the end of 1925 to provide the possibility of a new stabilization at a somewhat lower parity. A new bank of issue had been created which was at least legally independent of the government. There had been a return of internal, if not external, confidence and a large part of this confidence still remained at the end of 1925. The Grabski attempt also left several legacies that would be important in the next stabilization attempt. The Federal Reserve Bank of New York had, through the extension of a credit that was to run until the summer of 1926, acquired an interest in Polish monetary affairs; and the Bank of Poland had learned that it would find a sympathetic ear in New York. On the other hand, the experience had left some feeling of dissatisfaction on the part of the Polish government with the firm of Dillon, Read and Company as its financial agent. Whether or not the blame for the failure to issue the full $50-million loan in the spring of 1925 can be laid at the door of Dillon, Read is not relevant. The important fact is that the Polish government had a feeling that its bankers had not done all that they might have done. Finally, Grabski's failure left a realization of the need for a carefully prepared program to serve as a basis for the next stabilization attempt.

On November 20, 1925, Grabski was replaced by George Zdziechowski as Finance Minister. Zdziechowski immediately announced his intention of halting, during the first quarter of 1926, the issue of subsidiary notes and coins. On the advice of Dillon, Read and Company, the Polish government invited Professor E. W. Kemmerer of Princeton University, a noted American banking expert, to study the Polish situation. After a two-week stay in Poland, Kemmerer presented a number of rather generalized recommendations on Jan-

20 Chandler, *Benjamin Strong, Central Banker*, p. 391.

uary 9 and 10, 1926. The most significant of these was his advice that Poland should attempt to stabilize the zloty at par before prices and wages had had an opportunity to adjust to a depreciated value.[21] Little was done to implement these recommendations, however, and the zloty continued to decline through the spring of 1926. As a result of the submission of these recommendations, on the other hand, an exchange of correspondence between Zdziechowski and Kemmerer was initiated which led to the extension of another invitation to Kemmerer to organize a commission to undertake a more thorough study of the Polish economy. The invitation was later confirmed by the Pilsudski government and the Kemmerer mission spent a large part of the summer of 1926 in Poland.[22] It was on the basis of the very exhaustive reports of this commission that the Polish Plan of Stabilization was constructed. Of particular interest is the fact that Kemmerer no longer recommended an attempt to bring the zloty back to parity. He now recommended stabilization at a rate of 9 zlotys to the dollar, which would correspond to the prevailing market rate in the summer of 1926.[23]

Thus, Kemmerer seemed to share the central bankers' conviction that stabilization must be essentially at the prevailing market rate. In the Polish case, however, the market rate had been essentially market determined and an examination of post-stabilization price behavior seems to indicate that this rate was approximately correct for stabilization. With respect to Poland, it is even more difficult than usual to make any meaningful purchasing power parity calculations. There is no postwar year, at least prior to stabilization, in which one can reasonably assume that the relationship between Polish and world prices had reached equilibrium. On the other hand, a prewar price index for Poland is virtually meaningless.[24] But a comparison of relative price movements indicates that the selected rate was internationally approximately correct. Wholesale price and cost

---

[21] Republic of Poland, *Reports submitted by the Commission of the American Financial Experts headed by Dr. E. W. Kemmerer* (Warsaw, 1926), pp. 553–55.

[22] *Ibid.*, pp. iii–iv.   [23] *Ibid.*, pp. 19–21.

[24] Nevertheless, the Polish postwar indices of wholesale prices and cost of living given in the *Statistical Yearbook of the League of Nations 1930/31* are given on a base of 1913 and 1914 respectively. For calculations of percentage change, however, the choice of base year is unimportant.

of living indices for the United States, United Kingdom, and Poland for the years 1927, 1929, and 1931 are given below: [25]

Wholesale Price Index

Year	United States	United Kingdom	Poland
1927	137	142	119
1929	138	137	113
1931	106	105	87.5

Cost of Living Index

Year	United States	United Kingdom	Poland
1927	162	164	115
1929	162	163	123
1931	142	147	104

Movements of these indices in the periods 1927–1929 and 1927–1931 were as follows:

Wholesale Prices

Country	1927–1929	1927–1931
United States	+0.7%	−22.6%
United Kingdom	−3.5%	−26.0%
Poland	−5.0%	−26.5%

Cost of Living

Country	1927–1929	1927–1931
United States	0%	−12.3%
United Kingdom	−0.6%	−10.4%
Poland	+7.0%	−9.6%

The discussion on page 36 above concerning the difficulties involved in using either 1929 or 1931 as terminal dates for the comparison of price level movements is as relevant to Polish price movements as it is to Belgian. Nevertheless, the data indicate that Polish prices moved essentially parallel with world prices, particularly over the

[25] Data are taken from the *Statistical Yearbook of the League of Nations 1930/31*, pp. 270–72 and 274–76, and the same yearbook for 1935/36, pp. 239–41 and 242–44.

longer time span. Thus it appears that Polish prices were not particularly influenced by an unbalanced exchange ratio.

One must recognize, however, that these calculations are based on *ex post* data. The Poles were faced with an *ex ante* problem and, as has been pointed out, purchasing power parity calculations were particularly difficult in the Polish case. Kemmerer's recommendation was not based solely on the fact that the market rate was approximately 9 zlotys to the dollar, but also on the belief that Polish prices had essentially adjusted to this rate. His recommendation was based on a careful study of relative price behavior. In the later negotiations, the Poles adopted Kemmerer's recommendation and the central bankers relied on his studies so that there was no serious question raised about the selected exchange value of the zloty.

In the spring of 1926, however, Kemmerer had not yet begun his studies and, even though the zloty was continuing its fall, the Polish government was still thinking in terms of a return to the Grabski parity of 5.18 zlotys to the dollar. Jan Ciechanowski, Polish Minister to the United States, visited Governor Strong on March 12, 1926, to inform Strong of the negotiations that had been going on with private bankers over various possibilities for floating a Polish loan. He advised Strong that Poland's financial and economic program had the following principal aims:

1. To effect in a period of six months an absolute balance of the budget through the gradual reduction of expenditures, especially in the item of military administration.
2. To stabilize the currency at par.
3. To reduce the rate of interest in short term credit transactions.
4. To re-establish long term credit.
5. To place the railway system not only on a self-supporting basis but on a basis which would bring revenue; at the same time building new railways and waterways.
6. To improve the present state of agriculture.[26]

Ciechanowski had been negotiating with the Bankers Trust Company over the possibility of issuing a loan based on leasing to them

[26] Memorandum for Governor Strong, April 8, 1926, prepared by Ciechanowski, Federal Reserve, Correspondence, Stabilization, Bank Polski, April 1926–August 1927.

the Polish Tobacco Monopoly. He was also negotiating with Dillon, Read and Company over the possibility of issuing the remaining $15 million of the 1925 loan. The negotiations with the Bankers Trust Company broke down, ". . . it having been found impossible by the Polish Government to agree to certain forms of financial control which the Bankers Trust Company desired to impose as a condition to the granting of such a loan." [27] Although negotiations with Dillon, Read were still continuing, agreement with them was never, in fact, reached.

Already at this point, the Polish government was trying to avoid the League of Nations and the Bank of England. Ciechanowski summarized as follows his understanding of the views expressed by Strong during their conversation with respect to control of Polish finances by the League: "As regards foreign control of Poland's finances, you expressed the opinion that control by means of the League of Nations was, for various political and other reasons, undesirable for Poland." [28] This statement of his position was, however, a little too bald for Strong. He replied to Ciechanowski by saying:

As regards foreign control of Poland's finances by means of the League of Nations, the bare statement that this is undesirable for Poland is capable of considerable surmise as to the basis of that belief. Indeed, it might be the fact that, failing other arrangements, such plans would be desirable then, although possibly not now. In general, my point of view, based upon such knowledge as I now have, has been: first, that it would prove unacceptable to the Polish people; second, that it would be difficult, especially in this country, to dissociate such control from possible political objects, although no such objects were contemplated; and third, that such a control would be less satisfactory to American bankers and investors than would some other type of control having a less degree of political appearance.

This does not mean that my own attitude towards the splendid constructive work the League of Nations has done through the Financial Section is anything but appreciative. What has been done in Austria and in Hungary notably illustrates this, but as I stated to you, my personal impression is that such a procedure in the case of Poland would be less desirable than some other plan, if one could be found.[29]

27 *Ibid.*   28 *Ibid.*
29 Letter, April 19, 1926, Strong to Ciechanowski, Federal Reserve, Correspondence, Stabilization, Bank Polski, April 1926–August 1927.

Ciechanowski had pointed out at the March 12 meeting that the Polish government had been trying to obtain advice directly from Governor Strong and from Governor Norman. He and Strong had agreed in principle that it would be possible for Strong to coordinate his views with those of the Governor of the Bank of England thereby eliminating the need for the Polish government to negotiate directly with Norman.[30] Thus, the way was already being prepared to place the Bank of England in a secondary role. The reason, of course, was the awareness of Norman's conviction as to the necessity for League controls in the case of Poland. This reason, however, was not mentioned. Rather, Ciechanowski wrote:

I should like to make it clear that my Government have the greatest regard for the opinion of the Governor of the Bank of England and are anxious to enlist his support in the work towards the placing of Polish finances on a sound basis. I strongly feel, however, that for practical purposes it would facilitate matters if you could coordinate the views of Governor Norman with your own so as to enable us to conduct subsequent discussions through you, instead of discussing the same matters in New York and London at the same time. Such a method of procedure appears to me all the more practical in view of the fact that the Polish Government have decided to engage an American mission of financial expert advisors, and it would therefore be easier later to consult with these experts, should the necessity arise, on any matter of detail in New York than in London.[31]

This matter was followed up two months later when Strong was in London. He was approached by the Poles there to try to use his influence to win Norman away from the League program which the Poles considered impossible for them. Strong did discuss the subject with Norman and it seemed that an alternative to a League program might be found. The two agreed that there were three possibilities for control of Polish finances, to which Norman reacted as follows:

1. League action, which Norman favored although he admitted that action along these lines was impossible until after the fall meeting at the League and might not be possible then.

30 Memorandum for Governor Strong, April 8, 1926, prepared by Ciechanowski, *ibid.*
31 Letter, April 21, 1926, Ciechanowski to Strong, *ibid.*

2. Expand the Kemmerer Commission to include representatives of England, France, and Holland, as well as possibly Switzerland and Sweden and even Germany if the Poles could be persuaded to accept them. In principle, Norman did not object to this idea although he pointed out that it involved setting up an organization that already existed in the League.

3. A purely American action built around Kemmerer's report. Norman refused to associate himself with this plan since he considered that it would be ineffective.[32]

The need for relatively stringent controls in the case of Poland was rather forcefully underscored at precisely this moment by the Pilsudski *coup d'état*, which gave the Federal Reserve some bad moments, particularly over rumors of a government seizure of the gold stocks of the Bank of Poland.[33] This necessarily caused a temporary suspension of stabilization discussions, but the Pilsudski regime was quickly installed, confirmed the appointment of the Kemmerer Commission, and the way was prepared for reopening negotiations. But the Polish fears of the strict controls which they knew Norman would insist upon if he could is evident in their reaction to the possibility of converting the Kemmerer group into an international commission. Harrison met Ciechanowski on the train to Washington and wrote Strong about their conversation:

Incidentally, he had heard all about your talk with the Polish Minister at London and was quite opposed to your compromise suggestion about having various other nations represented on the Kemmerer commission. He said he took it up with Kemmerer, that he also was rather opposed, and

[32] Letter, May 15, 1926, Strong to Harrison, Harrison Collection, Box 15, Strong, Benjamin—European Trips (April 1926–September 1926).

[33] Harrison Collection, Binder 45. That fears of something of this sort did not end with the arrival of the Pilsudski government is indicated by the attitude of Stanislas Karpinski, President of the Bank of Poland, to the question of how much of the gold of the Bank of Poland should be held in its own vaults. After stabilization, the Bank of Poland was required to hold two-thirds of its gold backing in Poland, the other one-third being allowed to be held abroad. Karpinski fought this requirement because "the international and internal political situation of Poland is not such that one might wish to have more gold in Warsaw than in foreign countries" (undated memorandum covering discussions between Quesnay and Charles Dewey, Adviser under the Plan, over proposed changes in the presentation of the statement of the Bank of Poland, Federal Reserve, Correspondence, Poland, Bank of Poland Credit).

that he himself (I think) cabled Warsaw urging against it. He smiled and said that he thought that your suggestion was very probably out of deference to Norman. But I merely mentioned that I had not heard from you just what was the basis of your proposal. I assume, however, that as long as the Kemmerer commission is now all fixed, the Polish Government is going ahead with it on an American basis solely. Ciechanowski seems to think that the present set-up will facilitate credits in this country, will be just as satisfactory for credits in France as any compromise set-up, and that as far as London is concerned, they will not want to let the business go elsewhere when the time comes for a credit, regardless of who may have composed the commission mapping out the program.[34]

It is hardly possible to avoid the impression that the real interest of the Poles was the gaining of access to foreign financial markets with a minimum blow to their national pride and with the need to take unpopular internal measures reduced to the absolute minimum required to open those foreign markets. Such an attitude is perfectly understandable and acceptable provided that the internal measures demanded by the foreigners would be adequate to insure effective stabilization and that the measures would be conscientiously followed by the Poles. This need for the foreigners to impose some minimum conditions on Polish policy was not really recognized by the Poles, who concentrated only on their need for access to foreign funds.

The arguments of the Poles against international expansion of the Kemmerer mission, however, avoided stressing the increased severity of control which such an expansion was likely to entail. Rather, they tended to concentrate on the greater political acceptability, especially to the Polish people, of a purely American mission. Ciechanowski himself wrote Strong on July 14, 1926, to present his objections to the expansion. Those objections were that expansion of the mission would tend to make it unwieldy and lacking in coordination, that political bias would be present in some European financial experts, and that a purely American mission, being clearly nonpolitical, would be more acceptable to Polish public opinion.[35]

[34] Letter, June 18, 1926, Harrison to Strong, Strong Papers, Harrison to Strong, 1926-27.

[35] Letter, July 14, 1926, Ciechanowski to Strong, Federal Reserve, Poland, Stabilization, Bank Polski, April 1926-August 1927.

Strong, however, had apparently not taken the idea too seriously
himself. He wrote to Harrison with reference to Ciechanowski's and
Harrison's letters on the subject:

He need have no anxiety in regard to the suggestion discussed with the
Polish Minister in London, which was most tentative indeed and, as you
have surmised, more for the purpose of trying Norman as to his true position. While he is wedded to the League of Nations idea, I told him quite
frankly that I did not think we would be interested in any project along
lines similar to those employed in Austria and Hungary. The political atmosphere is too intense, and there is too much play for position through
the League, to justify our taking part. While he said that he would not
necessarily stand out from some plan composed by a commission with international representatives on it, he was not especially interested in any
plan produced under the auspices of the Kemmerer Commission and fathered by Dillon, Read & Co. Later, at Antibes, he rather withdrew from
what he had said in regard to a plan produced by an international commission. I think what lies behind the whole difficulty with Norman is his mistrust of Dillon Read & Co., basing that a good deal upon Logan's
performances.[36]

From the time that Pilsudski took over the Polish government the
zloty began to improve. Perhaps the promise of stability and forceful leadership which his strongman tactics brought played some part
in this improvement. More significant, however, was the fact that
the British coal strike began in May 1926 and led to heavy demands
for Polish coal. The result was a distinct improvement in Poland's
internal economic condition and a large increase in the value of Polish exports so that foreign exchange began to flow to the Bank of
Poland.[37] By the end of the summer, the zloty had been stabilized
de facto at about 9 zlotys to the United States dollar.

In July the Bank of Poland requested an extension of the Federal
Reserve credit for all or part of the $10 million and the Federal Re-
serve Bank of New York indicated a willingness to renew for a period of three months pending completion of the Kemmerer report,

36 Letter, August 3, 1926, Strong to Harrison, Strong Papers, European Trips.
James A. Logan was a European representative of Dillon, Read & Co. whose
personality and methods, for reasons which are not clear, seem to have aroused
considerable mistrust throughout banking circles.
37 Heilperin, Le Problème monétaire, p. 152.

provided only that Kemmerer approved.[38] The extension was not taken up by the Bank of Poland, however; in fact, the entire credit had been repaid by the end of August.

Poland's improved economic situation and the completion of the work of the Kemmerer Commission provided hope for a new stabilization attempt. The path for action was prepared by the passage of two laws on August 2, 1926, granting the President of the Republic the power to issue decrees having the force of law during the period when the Diet and Senate were not in session for the purposes of securing budget equilibrium and of stabilizing the currency. Such decrees, however, would lose their force if not submitted to the Diet within fourteen days after the opening of its next session or if declined by the Diet after having been submitted to it.[39] As the events occurred, the decrees issued under this authority were submitted to the Diet within the required period and were approved by it.

In September of 1926 Feliks Mlynarski was in London to discuss with Strong and with Norman and Siepmann of the Bank of England the possibility of credit extensions to the Bank of Poland. Strong told him that, since Kemmerer had gone to Poland under an arrangement worked out with Dillon, Read and Company, they would have to be the first to consider the report. Therefore, "I could give no intimation of our attitude at all in advance of seeing the report and consulting with Dillon, Read & Company, but I thought any discussion of credits was premature at this time." [40]

Mlynarski's report of his conversations with Norman and Siepmann ". . . indicated in substance that Norman appeared to be more friendly and sympathetic than he had been a year ago, but that both Norman and Siepmann had stated that Poland was just wasting time in fooling with the Kemmerer Commission and that the only way in which the matter could be handled in their opinion was at one bite either through the League of Nations or some other mixed control that might be compared to Gilbert's control over the

38 Harrison Collection, Binder 33.

39 John Foster Dulles, *Poland: Plan of Financial Stabilization, 1927* (New York, 1928), pp. 35–38.

40 Memorandum re: "Poland," September 16, 1926, Federal Reserve, Correspondence, Poland, Stabilization, Bank Polski, April 1926–August 1927.

German situation." [41] With respect to Strong's attitude, Mlynarski's report indicated that ". . . he got the impression that Governor Strong was not quite as interested as he had previously been in aiding Polish monetary reform and that he felt that Mr. Strong apparently wished to 'back off.' " [42] There is no other indication of a desire, at this time, on the part of Strong to escape from his involvement in the Polish affair. By the summer of 1927, however, one has the definite impression that he regretted the position of responsibility which the Federal Reserve Bank of New York had assumed, but no longer knew how to "back off."

In Mlynarski's discussions with Strong in September 1926, however, he certainly left no impression of a sympathetic reception at the Bank of England. Strong reported that portion of the conversations as follows:

He spoke of the very stern reception which he had had in the Bank of England, where very hostile things had been said about the Kemmerer mission. He said that he was acquainted with my discussions with Ciechanowski and the Polish Minister in London, and rather intimated that it might be up to me to have a talk with Governor Norman.

I told him that nothing in the conversations or correspondence that I had had, placed any obligation of that sort upon me. I had said that under suitable auspices, at a favorable moment, I would talk with Governor Norman, that I had done so when I was in London last May, had ascertained pretty clearly what his attitude was, and that the information had been reported back home and I understood had been given to the Polish Minister. I said that, in any event, that conversation was of no consequence, because at the very moment when I talked with the Minister in London and with Governor Norman, the revolution was taking place in Poland and no one could forecast the outcome of the revolution nor what the attitude of the foreign bankers would be as a result of it. [43]

Apparently both parties had forgotten the agreement of the previous spring whereby Strong had undertaken to coordinate the views of Norman and himself, while the Poles would confine their direct negotiations to dealing with Strong. The views of Norman and

[41] Harrison confidential memorandum to the files, November 5, 1926, subject: "Poland," *ibid.* The memorandum summarizes a conversation of that date which Harrison had with Ciechanowski.
[42] *Ibid.*   [43] Memorandum re: "Poland," September 16, 1926, *ibid.*

Strong could scarcely be considered coordinated, and the Poles were certainly dealing directly with both the Federal Reserve and the Bank of England. Nor were the Poles apparently telling quite the same story to both banks.

Mlynarski told Strong that Kemmerer's report was excellent and comprehensive and that the only point on which he differed with the conclusions was over Kemmerer's recommendation that a gold exchange standard be adopted. Mlynarski would have preferred a pure gold standard. Strong reports that he went on to say:

> that the report in principle would be adopted by the Government, but certain details might be modified or suspended from immediate operation. (This hardly gibes with what he said to Siepmann, who tells me that Mlynarski's attitude with him was that the Kemmerer mission was merely a facade, made for the purpose of advertising Poland in the United States and that they never really expected any thoroughgoing reorganization as a result of it, but only to overcome the hostility caused by propaganda conducted in America by some of the enemies of Poland.) [44]

In any event, Polish stabilization plans were much too vague to permit any concrete steps being taken at this time. Real preparatory measures began in December of 1926. Jean Monnet of the firm of Blair and Company went to Warsaw on the invitation of the Polish government in the middle of that month. He was advised that the Polish government no longer considered Dillon, Read and Company their bankers in New York and was asked for his advice and help regarding their stabilization program. He advised them that he did not see how they could stabilize effectively unless they provided for some sort of control which might insure confidence in Polish credit throughout the world. In fact, Monnet told Harrison that he advised them that some sort of control under the auspices of the League or a control similar to that of Gilbert under the Dawes Plan would be required and that the Poles had indicated a willingness to consider some such scheme if necessary.[45] Whether or not the proposition was put this clearly to the Poles is, however, open to some question. Governor Moreau was advised by Joseph Avenol, Deputy

[44] *Ibid.;* see pp. 69–71.
[45] Harrison memorandum to the Filing Department, February 2, 1927, subject: "Poland," Harrison Collection, Binder 58.

Secretary General of the League of Nations, on December 30, 1926, that, in Moreau's words, "des efforts sont faits en ce moment pour mettre un terme à la véritable tyrannie qu'exerce la Banque d'Angleterre sur les Banques d'Emission européenes." [At this moment, efforts are underway to put a stop to the veritable tyranny which the Bank of England exercises over European Banks of Issue.] Avenol advised in confidence that Monnet was preparing a plan for stabilizing the zloty without going to Norman.[46] It must be remembered that the French, including Avenol, considered the Financial Committee of the League of Nations as being essentially synonymous with the Bank of England. There seems no doubt, however, that Monnet did advise the Poles that some form of control would be required.

While in Warsaw, Monnet learned that the Poles were, at the same time as they were dealing with him, negotiating with the Bankers Trust Company regarding the handling of development loans in the American market. Both the Banker's Trust Company's representative and Monnet advised the Poles that stabilization was a necessary prerequisite to development loans. In fact, Blair and Company, Bankers Trust, and Chase Securities Corporation agreed at this time that they would all act together on any Polish business if the Polish government should wish them to do so.

Monnet also told Harrison that Mlynarski was very anxious to bring a commission representing the Polish government to New York to discuss stabilization problems with Governor Strong. Harri-

---

[46] Moreau, *Souvenirs*, p. 191. Another indication of Moreau's feelings about the Bank of England and the possibilities of any real cooperation between the Banks of France and England is given by another entry in Moreau's diary under the date of January 3, 1927: "Je reçois une lettre du gouverneur de la Banque de Yougoslavie me remerciant de l'offre que nous lui avons faite de servir à son établissement d'intermédiares avec la *Federal Reserve Bank* de New York. Du côté de Belgrade aussi, on essaie d'échapper aux visées impérialistes de M. Norman. Tous ces symptômes sont interressants. Ils prouvent que le relèvement de la France est suivi avec intérêt en Europe centrale, et que l'on supporte avec impatience le joug de l'Angleterre" [I just received a letter from the governor of the Bank of Yugoslavia thanking me for the offer we made to serve as intermediaries between his institution and the Federal Reserve Bank of New York. In Belgrade also, one attempts to escape the imperialist grip of Mr. Norman. All these symptoms are interesting. They prove that French recovery is followed with interest in central Europe, and that people suffer the yoke of England with impatience.] (*ibid.*, p. 192).

son pointed out that Strong could not receive an official delegation representing the Polish government but would be glad to discuss any matters with Mlynarski or any representative of the Bank of Poland at any time.[47]

In December of 1926 the Polish government entrusted Mlynarski and Professor Adam Krzyzanowski with the mission of securing American cooperation in a plan of stabilization. The two came to New York in February 1927 to work out the details of a plan with the private bankers and with the Federal Reserve Bank of New York. A rough plan that envisioned a loan issue of approximately $50 million was worked out and taken back to Poland for presentation to the Polish government and the Bank of Poland.[48] As drafted at this time, the plan provided for control to be exercised by an American Adviser and an international committee of experts on the directorate of the Bank of Poland, which was to consist of the Adviser plus an Englishman, a Frenchman, and a Swiss. The appointments were to be made by the Bank of Poland.[49]

Strong was at this time recuperating from illness in Biltmore, North Carolina; but he and Harrison immediately began to make plans for Harrison to travel to Europe in order to sound out Norman, Moreau, and Schacht about possible participation in a central bank credit in support of the program. Strong, of course, took a great interest in the trip and sent Harrison a long memorandum of advice as to how to proceed with each of the other principals. Above all, he stressed that Moreau must not be left with the feeling that things had been arranged with Norman and Schacht before Moreau had had an opportunity to express his views, and that Norman must not get the idea that the conclusion of a stabilization plan for Poland depended upon Norman's attitude.[50] The Federal Reserve Board was particularly concerned over the possibility that Harrison's trip might be interpreted as sponsoring a Federal Reserve

[47] Harrison memorandum to the Filing Department, February 2, 1927, subject: "Poland," Harrison Collection, Binder 58.

[48] J. F. Dulles, *Poland*, p. 3.

[49] Draft of Program of Stabilization, Federal Reserve, Correspondence, Bank Polski.

[50] Memorandum, March 9, 1927, Strong to Harrison, subject: "Approach re Polish Matter," Federal Reserve, Correspondence, Poland, Stabilization, Bank Polski, April 1926–August 1927.

Bank plan for Poland.[51] How some such interpretation could be avoided is difficult to see, but Harrison apparently felt that so long as there was no indication that the Federal Reserve was a co-author of the program, which they were not, or that it was formally sponsoring the program, this position could be avoided. The Board seemed to accept this view. In any case, Harrison sailed for Europe on March 18, 1927.

He went first to London and on March 29 cabled his initial impressions of Norman's views. He found Norman quite satisfied with the financial aspects of the program, but "he does question . . . whether you can sever the financial aspects of Poland's case from the political ones and that being so he seems loath to miss this opportunity to impose that form of control which will best insure political stability as well as financial stability." Still, Harrison had the impression that Norman would do his best to work out some generally acceptable solution. He summarized by saying:

. . . he wants stabilization in Poland, he sees the great advantage of acting now when the iron is hot, he thinks the proposed plan wholly satisfactory as a financial plan and says himself that he has no feasible suggestion at this time how to cover the point of international control which he has in mind. As to that I think he will be satisfied if Schacht is and if Schacht is not satisfied with plan as now formulated (as I rather imagine Norman suspects) that he will then sincerely do what he can toward facilitating a common viewpoint that will make possible unity of action by all the interested banks of issue. In a way that unity is more important to him than this particular problem.[52]

Harrison, however, evidently underestimated the depth of Norman's feeling about the failure to go through the League. The day after Harrison's cable was sent, Norman reported to the Committee of Treasury of the Bank of England that the Bank of England and New York might split over the difference of principle.[53]

Harrison proceeded to Paris where he discussed the program with Moreau, Rist, and Quesnay. Predictably, he found them in complete

[51] Letter, March 18, 1927, Harrison to Strong, *ibid.*
[52] Cable, March 29, 1927, Harrison to Case and Strong, Harrison Collection, Binder 34.
[53] Clay, *Lord Norman,* p. 259.

agreement with the program and eager to participate in a credit if asked. The one suggestion which they had was a surprising one coming from this source. That suggestion was that the plan should include some provision for international arbitration of disputed questions of control during the period of the program as well as of the question of continuation of controls beyond the initial period of three years.[54]

Schacht's initial reaction was somewhat more guarded, but he did express himself as being in favor of Polish stabilization and glad to cooperate with the other banks of issue in a stabilization program. He was certain, however, that the German government would not permit the floating of any part of the loan in Berlin since Poland had not yet ". . . recognized decree of Hague Court that certain German nationals ousted from Poland must be reimbursed for property taken and that a loan to Poland in such circumstances was an impossible thing to expect." He declined to pass upon the plan but agreed with Moreau's suggestion regarding provisions for arbitration. He expressed the view that the loan appeared to him unnecessarily large and that the bank of issue credit ". . . might on that account be misconstrued merely as a seal for bankers loan." [55]

The four central bankers met at Calais on April 3, 1927, to review the opinions they had expressed separately. All agreed that they would participate in a credit to the Bank of Poland if asked, provided:

(a) That as contemplated the program shall have been examined and formally approved with such amendments as might be necessary by a responsible international committee of experts
(b) That the program so approved shall have been legally adopted by the Polish Government in agreement with the private bankers and
(c) That any questions of dispute during the operation of the program concerning control or the continuation of control as provided for in the plan should be referred to some international mechanism for arbitration. For this mechanism Norman and Schacht would prefer League but Moreau and Rist believe impossible to get League as arbitrator not having fathered program.[56]

[54] Cable, April 5, 1927, Harrison to Strong and Case, Harrison Collection, Binder 34.
[55] *Ibid.*   [56] *Ibid.*

Both Norman and Schacht emphasized, however, that they did not want to assume responsibility in any way for the ultimate success of the loan of the private bankers nor to pass upon the program itself. In this connection they went so far as to express a preference for extending an unconditional loan to the Bank of Poland then rather than after adoption of the program. In this way, the banks of issue could not be held responsible in the minds of the public either for the program or for the loan. They also questioned whether it would be possible for the Bank of Poland to appoint an adequate international committee of experts unless the banks of issue assisted them in doing so. This too they were opposed to doing because it might make the banks of issue responsible for the acts of their appointees. Harrison summarized their views as follows:

Obviously Norman and Schacht do not want to be responsible for defeat of present efforts by any refusal to cooperate but having some doubts about proposed procedure (some of which are quite real in their minds while others are perhaps pique) they would prefer to put responsibility for this procedure on us if possible and thus agree to participate if we ask them to. I have not yet pressed the point whether they differentiate between being asked by us to participate and being asked by someone else to join if we do.[57]

But again, Harrison seems to have underestimated the extent of the mental reservations and annoyance on the part of both Norman and Schacht. It was only natural for Norman to feel piqued to see the control of European monetary affairs escaping from his control and Schacht had every political reason to be reluctant to be put in the position of aiding Polish recovery. These understandable, if perhaps not quite legitimate, concerns appear to have been aggravated by a belief that undue concessions were being made to Polish sensibilities and that the program was not being prepared with the thoroughness required. For example, during the course of the meetings, Schacht had raised the subject of German claims against Poland. Even Siepmann of the Bank of England, which was in general siding with the Reichsbank in these discussions, conceded that "in general, the German list of claims seems to be very various, easily disputable,

[57] *Ibid.*

difficult to assess, and only enforceable by the most elaborate legal proceedings, involving huge expense and endless delay. The practical bearing of these claims on any negotiations of the Polish Government for an international loan seems to be very remote." [58] Despite the fact that he had been given some information about these matters during the voyage to Europe, however, Harrison appears to have been caught somewhat unprepared with respect to these German claims. Immediately after the meetings, Norman sent him a note in which Norman indulged in a degree of sarcasm that was quite unusual in his dealings with the Federal Reserve Bank. He wrote: "The fact that you were not aware of the 'liquidation' liabilities of the Polish Government, to which reference was made the other day by Dr. Schacht, leads me to draw your attention to some other liabilities towards the Allied Goverments and the Reparation Commission, of which I enclose a summary statement." [59]

However hedged with qualifications and mental reservations, some sort of agreement in principle had been reached by the major central bankers and Harrison returned to New York. During the months of April and May 1927, representatives of the Polish government, the Bank of Poland, and the private bankers met in Paris to negotiate the stabilization loan. A particularly difficult problem was how an international committee could be appointed to review the plan as called for in the program. Schacht had already expressed doubts on this point, saying that he thought it very difficult, if not impossible, to have a suitable committee appointed either by the borrower or the lender.[60] By May 4, 1927, the group in Paris had come to the conclusion that it was absolutely essential to drop this requirement. A cable to this effect was sent to the Federal Reserve with the suggestions that the Federal Reserve designate experts to examine the plan unofficially and that it designate Governor Moreau to represent it in Paris during the negotiations. The Federal Reserve reacted coolly to both suggestions.[61] Still, the idea of an in-

[58] Letter, April 8, 1927, Siepmann to Harrison, Federal Reserve, Correspondence, Poland, Stabilization, Bank Polski, April 1926–August 1927.
[59] Letter, April 7, 1927, Norman to Harrison, *ibid.*
[60] Letter, April 30, 1927, Schacht to Harrison *ibid.*
[61] Moreau, *Souvenirs,* pp. 301–304. Moreau was quite disappointed with New York's cool reply. He commented in his diary: "On ne veut pas solliciter le

ternational review committee got dropped from the plan although it was not clearly spelled out what, if anything, was to take its place.

Another difficult problem arose over the issue of arbitration in the event of disagreement between the Adviser, the Bank of Poland, and the Polish government. The essence of the problem was stated in a cable from the Bankers Trust Company to its representative in Paris following a conference that had been held at the Federal Reserve Bank of New York.

Federal felt and still feels that the original scheme of four international members of Bank Polski of which three would act as arbitrators was soundest method. Apparently you have discarded that feature of plan which they and we consider unfortunate. If however you believe Poles unwilling to put that back into program then countersuggestion is that government agree at this time that for purposes of arbitration they will call on representatives of neutral banks of issue for instance Holland, Sweden and Switzerland. Perhaps the Advisory Committee suggested in section four of latest draft might serve this purpose. The other banks of issue laid special stress on the point of control and arbitration and as far as Federal knows have never changed their attitude.[62]

The Advisory Committee referred to grew out of the elimination of the provision for four foreign directors on the Board of the Bank of Poland. The final plan provided for only an American director who would be also the Adviser to the government. He was empowered to create an Advisory Committee of Financial Experts to sit under his chairmanship.[63] Under the plan, however, this committee was not responsible for preliminary review and, in fact, was only to be created after the plan was implemented and if the Adviser felt a need for it. It was not given any arbitration functions, rather the

---

concours de la Banque de France ni prendre de responsabilités. La mentalité américaine me paraît faite de scrupules et de complications qui s'accordent mal avec l'action." [They don't want to solicit the cooperation of the Bank of France nor accept responsibility. It seems to me that the American mentality is made up of scruples and complications which are incompatible with action.]

[62] Bankers Trust Company cable, May 19, 1927, Tompkins to Close, Federal Reserve, Correspondence, Poland, Stabilization, Bank Polski, April 1926–August 1927.

[63] Plan of Stabilization in J. F. Dulles, *Poland,* p. 20. By letter of July 6, 1927, to Mlynarski, Dulles and Denis (counsel and representative, respectively, of the bankers) confirmed the understanding that the Committee was to advise the American Director and not the government, the bank, or its board (*ibid.,* p. 24).

plan specified that "in case of any disagreements arising under the Plan between the Government and the Adviser, each will appoint a representative and the two will endeavor to adjust the difference. If they should not succeed the two representatives will agree on a third party of different nationality, as arbitrator whose decision shall be final." [64]

The plan, as finally approved by the Polish government, provided for a foreign loan of about $60 million. Of this amount, $15 million was to be used for purposes of economic development, about $25 million was to be used to retire outstanding Treasury notes, about $3 million to retire Treasury floating debt, about $8.5 million to increase the capital of the Bank of Poland, and about $8.5 million as Treasury reserve.[65] The security for service of the loan was to be the customs revenues of Poland, which were to be held in a special account releasable only by the Adviser, who was also to be the representative of the Fiscal Agents for the loan. In addition, the proceeds of the loan would be paid in to the Bank of Poland and would only be released on authorization of the Adviser.[66] Thus, as representative of the Fiscal Agents, the powers of the Adviser were adequate to protect the bond holders—at least so long as the Polish government and the Bank of Poland abided by the terms of the agreement which, in fact, they did do. With respect to general control over Polish fiscal and monetary policies, his powers were much more vague and limited. In this capacity, his authority was limited to that of a rather special member of the Board of Directors of the bank and to the furnishing of advice to the government, advice which could be accepted or not as the government saw fit. The greatest weakness of his position, as compared with the Reparations Agent in Germany or the Commissioners-General in Austria and Hungary, was that there was no recognized international body behind him to which appeal could be made in case events should develop in a way which to him signaled danger. Since he was not appointed by an outside agency, he was in the awkward position of being responsible to the very institutions which he was supposed to control.

Despite the insistence of Norman and Schacht that they did not wish to pass upon the program itself and would only participate in a

[64] *Ibid.*, p. 21.   [65] *Ibid.*   [66] *Ibid.*, pp. 22–23.

credit on the simple basis that they had been asked to do so by another bank of issue (and presumably only if the request were from the Federal Reserve Bank of New York), the Federal Reserve authorities of the time were already trying to escape their responsibility in the matter. On May 18, 1927, Close and Monnet in Paris cabled as follows to the Bankers Trust Company in New York:

The Federal Reserve having assumed leadership must retain it as none of the other banks would be willing to appear in the slightest degree to desire to take over a leadership which has been definitely assumed by the Federal Reserve. The Bank of France is exceedingly desirous of seeing the plan consummated and would be willing if asked to assume with the Federal Reserve a definite responsibility for the soundness of the monetary aspects of the plan and also if asked to collaborate with the Federal Reserve in organizing the credit. The Bank of England ānd the Reichsbank do not wish to be consulted with reference to the plan itself but will be glad to participate in a credit if asked by the Federal Reserve Bank. You will appreciate that this attitude is in accordance with the precedent established in the arrangement of other stabilization credits where one of the Banks of Issue has assumed the leadership and the special responsibility incident thereto. . . . The Banque de France would have been willing to represent the Federal Reserve Bank in passing on the details of the monetary features of the plan if definitely requested. The Bank felt however that Harrison's communications while raising no objections to the bank passing on monetary features of plan do not evidence a whole hearted desire that it should do so. The bank is of course most anxious not to do anything which might be construed as a desire to take away the leadership of the Federal Reserve and feels that in the interest of Poland and the success of the plan as a whole and to secure cooperation of other issuing banks the leadership should be such as to give no grounds of suspicion that the well known political friendship of France for Poland could in any way have affected their judgment on the plan. The bank is however prepared on the request of the Federal Reserve Bank to act in any capacity which the Federal Reserve Bank feels will assist it in consummating the plan.[67]

The next day, Strong cabled Moreau as follows:

Cables exchanged between the private bankers in Paris and New York seem unduly to emphasize the question of Central bank leadership and purport to indicate a willingness on the part of some of the banks of issue

[67] Cable, May 18, 1927, Close and Monnet to Bankers Trust Co., Federal Reserve, Correspondence, Bank Polski Credit, Cables.

to participate solely upon our request that they participate rather than upon their own judgment of the merits of the whole matter. This would place us too much in the position of assuming all the responsibility for the form of the plan as well as its subsequent execution and success and does not fairly reflect our views of the desirability of complete Central bank cooperation which we discussed at length in various meetings abroad.[68]

It seems evident that Strong's concern and that of the Federal Reserve Board was that the Reserve was in danger of becoming too embroiled in Polish affairs to be compatible with the United States government's policy of isolation. But it was too late at this stage to disclaim responsibility for the program. The Federal Reserve had, in fact, assumed leadership and Norman and Schacht had made perfectly clear, not only that they were willing to participate on the sole basis of New York's request, but that this was the only basis on which they would be willing to participate. If the Federal Reserve authorities were unwilling to take responsibility for the program, they must be willing to see the program fail. If they were going to require Norman and Schacht to pass on the program, they had a moral obligation to make clear that they considered that others were free to refuse to join the consortium if unsatisfied with the program. In fact, the Federal Reserve pleaded its non-responsibility at the same time that it urged participation in the interests of "central bank cooperation."

The fact that the final negotiations with the private bankers, which resulted in some significant changes in the stabilization plan, took place in Paris without the presence there of a representative of the Federal Reserve Bank of New York inevitably meant some loss of control on the part of the Federal Reserve authorities. In view of the position of leadership which the Federal Reserve had clearly assumed, it is difficult to understand why it did not insist upon the negotiations taking place in New York or did not dispatch a top level representative to Paris. As it was, the Bank of France was left as the representative of the central bankers at the site of the negotiations and, apart from its acknowledged political interest in Polish affairs, it was handicapped by a reluctance to appear to usurp Federal Reserve leadership. From the point of view of the Bank of France,

[68] Cable, May 19, 1927, Strong to Moreau, *ibid.*

however, this may well not have been a handicap. It was left in a position such that, in the absence of objection from the Federal Reserve, it could permit matters to develop as it and the Poles wished without assuming responsibility for the consequences. This state of affairs continued until early June 1927.

On June 2, 1927, the Bank of Poland formally asked the Federal Reserve Bank of New York if it would be prepared to discuss the terms and conditions of a credit.[69] On June 7 Strong cabled Norman to advise him of this request and to outline his general idea of the credit terms which were, as he saw it, to follow the Belgian example in so far as possible. He advised Norman that the Bank of France had been requested to send a copy of the stabilization program to the Bank of England and asked if Norman, after reviewing the program, would cable whether or not the Bank of England would participate.[70] Norman replied by cable the next day, saying, "Without waiting to review program and merely repeating what was said a couple of months ago to Harrison I will recommend Bank of England to accept your invitation to participate in any such credit provided similar invitation is offered to and accepted by Reichsbank as well as Bank of France."[71] Strong and Norman discussed the matter by telephone and, somehow, Norman was led to accept the idea that his participation would be based on an examination of the plan.[72] The Federal Reserve requested the Bank of France to approach the other European banks of issue, except for the Bank of England, and to work out the details of their participation.[73] This was the first time that the Bank of France was put in the formal position of co-responsibility with the Federal Reserve and it was a limited and nebulous responsibility. Nevertheless, the Bank of France moved energetically and, after some delay in securing a final commitment from Norman and Schacht, the agreement was concluded on June 17, 1927.[74]

[69] Cable, June 2, 1927, Mlynarski to Harrison, *ibid.*
[70] Cable, June 7, 1927, Strong to Norman, *ibid.*
[71] Cable, June 8, 1927, Norman to Strong, *ibid.*
[72] Cable, June 9, 1927, Strong to Norman, *ibid.* The cable read in part: "As stated by telephone we now understand you will examine the plan so as to give your cooperation after considering its merits and not have us appear on the record as assuming full responsibility for your participation."
[73] Moreau, *Souvenirs*, p. 343.   [74] *Ibid.*, pp. 351–53.

The credit was to be in the total amount of $20 million for a period of one year. Its becoming effective was contingent upon arranging legal authority for the Bank of Poland to guarantee bills discounted, receipt of written assurance of the Polish government that it would interpose no obstacle to repayment even in gold if necessary, issue of the loan, and legal promulgation of final stabilization.[75] The terms and conditions were essentially those of the Belgian credit except that there were no special clauses providing separate interest rate provisions for the Federal Reserve Bank of New York.

A combination of circumstances forced a postponement of the issue of the loan, however. The New York bond market was weak at the moment and had been rather thoroughly saturated with foreign issues. More importantly, the assassination of a Russian official in Warsaw led to serious fears of Polish-Russian difficulties, so that the time was hardly propitious for the issue of a Polish loan even if the market had been strong.[76] For psychological reasons, however, it was felt that the Polish government should make some sort of public announcement. Not knowing when market conditions would make

[75] Cable, June 25, 1927, Moreau to Strong, Harrison Collection, Binder 27. It was originally specified that the conditions had to be met by August 20, 1927, or the credit offer would expire. When the loan issue could not be made until after that date, the time limit was extended to November 1, 1927. Participation in the credit, which was the same as the later actual participation, was as follows (all in gold currency equivalents):

Austria	$ 500,000
Belgium	500,000
Czechoslovakia	500,000
Denmark	250,000
Finland	250,000
France	3,000,000
Germany	3,000,000
Great Britain	3,000,000
Hungary	500,000
Italy	1,500,000
Netherlands	1,000,000
Sweden	250,000
Switzerland	500,000
United States	5,250,000

[76] Cable exchanges, June 14–24, 1927, between Tompkins, Bankers Trust Co., and Close in Warsaw, Federal Reserve, Correspondence, Bank Polski Credit, Cables.

possible an announcement of the loan issue, it was decided that the private bankers would extend a six-month credit to the Polish government in the amount of $15 million. It was orginally planned that the credit would be paid off out of the proceeds of the loan issue when the issue was made. Harrison objected to this, however, because it left the impression that the bond issue was being used to "bail out" the credit. Even if use of the credit were restricted to purposes specified in the stabilization plan, that portion of the proceeds of the loan used to repay the credit would not be applied directly to the purposes provided for in the plan. In this case, Harrison feared that some of the banks of issue might consider themselves released from the credit. The suspicion is strong that some of them might have welcomed such a convenient escape. To avoid this difficulty, however, the credit was instead secured by existing Treasury reserves so that there would be no direct connection between the credit and the loan.[77]

By July 7, 1927, all documents regarding the stabilization program and loan had been signed and all that remained to be settled was the date on which the loan issue should be made and the issue price of the bonds.[78] But the program almost fell apart over this apparently simple matter. Final negotiations with the bankers over the issue of the loan began in Warsaw in September. The original plan had been that the bonds would be thirty-three-year 7 per cent bonds redeemable at 105. The bankers now proposed an issue price of 90, which the Polish government flatly refused to accept. It insisted upon an issue price of 92, which the bankers felt would make successful flotation impossible.[79] Negotiations were suspended by the Poles, and on September 30, 1927, Strong cabled Moreau as follows:

I am disturbed to hear that the Polish Government has terminated negotiations with the American bankers. Am informed that the Government in-

[77] Harrison memorandum to the files, June 30, 1927, subject: "Bank of Poland," Federal Reserve, Correspondence, Poland, Stabilization, Bank Polski, April 1926–August 1927.

[78] Cable, July 7, 1927, Mlynarski to Strong, *ibid.*

[79] Memorandum, September 29, 1927, Harrison to Strong, subject: "Bank of Poland," Federal Reserve, Correspondence, Stabilization Credit, Bank Polski, September 1927–July 1928. Harrison closed his memorandum saying: "The whole thing is in a jolly good mess and worst of all indicates a certain ineptness and lack of foresight on the part of the Poles that is perhaps more discouraging than anything else."

sisted upon an issue price of 92 for a 33 year 7 per cent bond. To meet this the bankers reduced the proposed redemption price from 105 to 103 which did not satisfy the Government. The bankers state that the Government demands this price believing it should now realize a greater return because of the security and supervision and character of the plan. The Poles seem to overlook (a) that the present 8 per cent Polish loan is selling in our market at par and is redeemable at 105 which is approximately 8¼ per cent basis whereas the new loan at 90 is about 7.9 per cent basis, (b) that the issue price is really not fixed by the bankers but by the market and (c) that the present market value of the 8 per cent loan and the corresponding price of the present loan does in fact realize for the Polish Government all of the improvement which they can expect in their credit at this time as the 8 per cent bonds have advanced from the low of 86 in December 1925 to the present price of par largely because of the improvement which has already taken place in Poland and the prospect of the plan succeeding. Further benefits to their credit on this account will likely be realized only after the execution of their program.

I have made private inquiries in best quarters as to reasonableness of offering price and am assured that it is about right and that at any higher price the loan might not prove successful. In fact even at 90 there will be considerable difficulty in floating it. The impression resulting in this market from the failure of the plan will be most unfortunate. As matters now stand I would hesitate to recommend to our associates either a continuance of the credit or the establishment of a new one for the Bank Polski as part of some new program, under other auspices, as I fear that any terms for a bond issue which would be satisfactory to the Polish Government would on the other hand likely fail in the market.

Would appreciate a prompt expression of your views and am sending open message to save time.[80]

Moreau replied on October 1, 1927, that he shared Strong's views but that there was nothing to be done but await the results of the negotiations since they had always agreed that any interference by banks of issue in such negotiations was impossible.[81] The impasse was finally overcome by converting the bond issue into a twenty-year 7 per cent bond issued at 92 and callable at 103.[82] The loan agreement was signed on October 13, 1927, and the stabilization decree is-

[80] Cable, September 30, 1927, Strong to Moreau, Federal Reserve, Bank Polski Credit, Cables.

[81] Cable, October 1, 1927, Moreau to Strong, *ibid.*

[82] Cable, October 10, 1927, Bankers Trust Co., Chase Securities Corp., Blair & Co., and Guaranty Trust Co. to their agents in Warsaw, *ibid.* The Polish government realized only 86 on the bonds, however, since there was a 6-point spread deductible.

sued the same day. The loan was issued a few days later [83] and the central bank credit became effective October 18, 1927.

As far as the central bankers were concerned, the principal point of difficulty in the negotiations centered around the question of the adequacy of controls, particularly over the actions of the Polish government. The light in which the Polish government viewed the position of the Adviser is evidenced by a letter, signed by Marshal Pilsudski, which was handed to the bankers at the time of the signing of the final agreement on October 13, 1927. Shockingly enough, no objection seems to have been raised to the letter, a translation of which reads as follows:

> Considering that the interests of the borrower, that is to say of the State contracting to borrow for many years and which must repay the loan by means of taxes, and the interests of the creditor, that is to say of the banks, are entirely mutual when it is a question of the success of the loan distributed to the public—I believe that care to avoid conflicts and long debates (a source of discord) with respect to every detail is part of the mutual obligations.
>
> In view of all this, I decided upon signing the loan contracts to have handed to the representatives of the banks granting the loan my wish addressed to their delegate in Poland who will be attached as Adviser to our bank of issue. Desiring to avoid the consequences of conflicts and disputes, I express my wish [volonté] that the Adviser should abstain from reading Polish and German newspapers. The former serve the interests of parties which, having to deal with an impartial government, try to weaken governmental action by discovering a catastrophe in Poland at least once a week —a catastrophe which the government has not prevented or even which it has itself provoked. The German newspapers, for their part, imagine catastrophes for Poland at every moment, making Poland appear as a completely catastrophic State, impossible to control because the Polish atmosphere is saturated with the essence of catastrophe. In this way, the Adviser would avoid poor and erroneous information, the correction of which would take all of the Government's time without leaving it a minute of rest after its work.

[83] The total nominal amount was about $72 million, issued as follows:

England	£2,000,000
France	$2,000,000
Holland	$4,000,000
Poland	$1,000,000
Sweden	$2,000,000
Switzerland	$6,000,000
United States	$47,000,000

Furthermore, I desire that the Adviser should endeavor to avoid mixing in any manner whatever in the internal affairs of the State by undertaking to defend any party or group [coterie], and that he should be careful, in the economic and financial area, never to put himself in opposition to the Minister of Finance and the President of the Cabinet.

In expressing these desires, I have in mind the need to avoid conflicts and discords, and I do so knowing the excess of easy judgments and criticisms directed against Poland by foreigners.[84]

A letter expressing similar views in much more diplomatic language was also sent to the Adviser-designate by Ciechanowski. Ciechanowski particularly stressed that "whatever analogy may actually exist between your work as Adviser in Poland and such activities as those of Mr. S. Parker Gilbert in Germany, or Jeremiah Smith in Hungary, I consider it is important for you to avoid stressing any such analogy." [85]

The previous spring, Parker Gilbert had reviewed an early draft of the stabilization program from the vantage point of his position as Agent-General in Germany under the Dawes Plan. At that time, the position of the Adviser was even somewhat stronger than it was in the final version of the plan. It was then still planned that the program would be reviewed by an international committee of experts prior to implementation. In addition to the Adviser, it was expected that there would be three additional foreign members of the Board of Directors of the Bank of Poland. Under this provision, one-fourth of the expanded Board of the bank would have consisted of foreign Directors who might have been expected, in general, to support the Adviser vis-à-vis both the bank and the government. Both of these provisions were dropped in the course of the Paris negotiations in April and May. One cannot help but suspect that he sees the hand of the Bank of France in these changes. It is highly unlikely that Governor Moreau, or any of his representatives, took a direct part in these negotiations, which were between the Poles and the private bankers. But it is evident from Moreau's diary that he maintained close contact with the private bankers, particularly through Jean Monnet. There was nothing at all unusual in this; both Norman

84 Letter, October 13, 1927, signed by Pilsudski, Federal Reserve, Poland, Stabilization Credit, Bank Polski, September 1927–July 1928.
85 Letter, November 5, 1927, Ciechanowski to Dewey, ibid.

and Strong kept themselves well informed in comparable cases and did not hesitate to express their views when they felt that matters were progressing unsatisfactorily. In fact, this is precisely the task for which the Federal Reserve authorities should have had a representative in Paris during the negotiations. The point is that, since Strong did not properly provide for the execution of his responsibilities, the Bank of France was left with a free hand to influence the nature of the solutions arrived at. Very likely, it played a considerable part in determining the form that changes in the draft plan took.

It was to be expected that the Poles would try to make the controls specified by the plan as innocuous as possible. Moreau freely conceded that the Bank of France could at least be considered by others as being in a position to want to further French political interests in Poland, and it is reasonable to expect that it at least wanted to avoid damaging those interests. It was quite logical, then, to expect Moreau to support Polish efforts to ease the stringency of the control mechanism. After his meeting with Harrison on March 30, 1927, Moreau noted approvingly in his diary:

Il ne prévoit qu'un contrôle assez lâche sur la Banque de Pologne, en tout cas beaucop moins serré que celui établi par le Comité financier de la Société des Nations sur l'Allemagne, l'Autriche et la Hongrie, qui sont astreintes à payer des réparations, ce qui n'est pas le cas de la Pologne.[86] [He anticipates only a rather loose control over the Bank of Poland, in any case much less severe than that established by the Financial Committee of the League of Nations over Germany, Austria, and Hungary, who are forced to pay reparations, which is not the case with Poland.]

The private bankers had always insisted upon the necessity for adequate controls as a prerequisite to handling a stabilization loan, and it is doubtful if they would have agreed to relaxation of the already feeble position of the Adviser if they had been energetically supported by the central bankers. But at this point, the representative of the central bankers on the scene was Governor Moreau, whose sympathies were with the Poles and who was not to be considered as a responsible leader.

[86] Moreau, *Souvenirs*, p. 269.

In any event, when he reviewed this draft plan, Parker Gilbert commented:

I have naturally examined the draft program for Poland from the point of view of the external control that it provides, and particularly from the point of view of the proposed Adviser. Much will depend, of course, on the personality of the Adviser. I do not know whether there is anyone under consideration, but I should think it was by all means necessary to avoid getting a professor. What is needed is a practical man of affairs. . . .

One trouble that I see from the point of view of the Adviser is that his powers under the terms of the proposed plan are rather hazy and even a little ambiguous. . . . As I understand the present draft, the actual power of the Adviser would depend almost entirely on his control over the proceeds of the proposed loan, and even here he gets effective control only over part of the proceeds. . . .

Another serious defect in the Adviser's control is the absence of any outside authority to which recourse may be had in case of dispute between him and the Polish Government. At the very least there ought to be some provision for arbitration. I can quite understand that the Polish Government would not welcome anything like League of Nations control, but I have none the less supposed that it might be possible to safeguard the program of stabilization by providing in certain cases for appeals to a body like the Finance Committee of the League of Nations. The chances are that with a good Adviser there would never have to be many such appeals, but the mere existence of the right of appeal would have a healthy effect on the operation of the plan as a whole. If it is distasteful to the Poles to have the League of Nations brought into the plan even to this extent, it might perhaps be possible to use the proposed Special Committee of Directors of the Bank Polski for substantially the same purpose. This would be better than nothing, though it is not entirely satisfactory. If anything like this were to be done, it would seem it be desirable at the same time to enlarge the Special Committee to include a few more foreign members. . . .[87]

The final version of the plan limited the provisions for appeal to the question of arbitration and the provisions were such as to almost insure that the arbitrators would not be disinterested or unbiased.

Despite what was logically to be expected, no difficulties over control actually developed in practice. Gilbert had pointed out that much depended upon the personality of the Adviser. The man fi-

[87] Letter, April 5, 1927, Gilbert to Norman, Federal Reserve, Correspondence, Poland, Stabilization, Bank Polski, April 1926–August 1927.

nally selected for the position, Charles S. Dewey, had been a private banker in Chicago for a number of years and had been an Assistant Secretary of the United States Treasury at the time of his appointment. Strong had some doubts about him because of his lack of international experience, but he was selected when it was found that the first choice, Leon Fraser, was unavailable.[88] The absence of any difficulties in connection with the exercise of controls would seem to indicate that Dewey had the type of personality that Gilbert had in mind when stressing the importance of this factor.

Gilbert must have had in mind, however, the kind of man who could make control effective without arousing sufficient hostility to require resort to outside appeals. The lack of difficulty, on the other hand, seems to have been largely a result of Dewey's reluctance to force unpopular measures on the Poles. Already in May of 1928, Strong, after a dinner at the Bank of France at which he had talked with the Polish Ambassador to France and his wife, commented that ". . . they were so enthusiastic in their praise of Dewey that it raised some little question in my mind as to whether he had not been a little too much 'adopted' by the Poles and a little too inclined to accept the Polish point of view about the various problems he was dealing with." [89] A few months later, Dewey visited Strong at Evian-les-Bains and Strong commented:

> I was a little bit impressed with the idea that he may be somewhat more busy on Polish matters than is justified by his official relation to their affairs, but they seem to like him, and Dr. Schacht, who had opportunity to make some inquiries, said that he had gained the impression that Dewey was sympathetic but firm when necessary. I was a little disappointed to hear him so frequently refer to Polish matters as "our" problem or "our" affair. He seems to consider himself just as much a Pole as though he were born there. . . .
>
> On the whole, my talk with him left a favorable impression, but I dread a little bit the extent and character of some of his activities and the feeling of paternity which he seems to have developed about Poland and all of its 30 million people. . . .
>
> The plan of stabilization provides for segregation and independent oper-

[88] Cable, September 21, 1927, Strong to Moreau, Federal Reserve, Correspondence, Bank Polski Credit, Cables.

[89] Memorandum re: "Poland," May 24, 1928, Strong Papers, European Trips, 1928.

ation of the railways, somewhat along the lines of Belgium and Switzerland. This, he thinks, would be a mistake and there is strong opposition to it, particularly in military circles. I pointed out to him that, after all, the terms of the plan made it an obligation upon Poland to conclude this change, and I thought it would be a mistake to encourage them to neglect it. . . .[90]

The loan proceeds, as well as the writing up of existing assets of the Bank of Poland, raised its cover ratio to 110 per cent in December 1927;[91] and as early as November 1927 Norman and Strong had reason to question among themselves what they considered to be the excessive gold purchases of the Bank of Poland.[92] Despite this apparent strength and the fact that Polish stabilization was maintained beyond the period of general collapse in 1931, there were elements in the post-stabilization experience which indicate that the absence of discord over controls can hardly be attributed to the fact that all was well. The stabilization bonds sagged almost immediately after issue, largely as a result of the outbreak of border conflict between Poland and Lithuania. The bankers supported the market for a time and attempted to interest the Polish government in anticipating the first year's sinking fund payments so as to participate equally with the bankers in support of the market. The government declined, however, and support was withdrawn.[93] Nor was the market position of the bonds strengthened by Polish municipal borrowing in the spring of 1928 and rumors of other borrowings.[94] It is true that the Adviser had no authority to prevent such borrowing, since the government was only obligated to the extent that ". . . before authorizing any external loan guaranteed by the Government or any

90 Letter, July 16, 1928, Strong to Harrison, Federal Reserve, Correspondence, Poland, Stabilization Credit, Bank Polski, September 1927–July 1928.

91 Letter, December 5, 1927, Dewey to Strong, *ibid.* The statement of the bank was rearranged so as to reduce the apparent cover to 70 per cent by carrying some of the devisen in reserve accounts not shown as cover.

92 Letter, November 4, 1927, Norman to Strong, and letter, November 16, 1927, Strong to Norman, Strong Papers, Bank of England.

93 Letter, December 2, 1927, Ciechanowski to Harrison, and cable, December 8, 1927, from Czechowicz through Ciechanowski, Federal Reserve, Correspondence, Poland, Stabilization Credit, Bank Polski, September 1927–July 1928.

94 By March 1928, the City of Warsaw had borrowed $10 million and the City of Poznan $2.5 million. In addition, there were rumors, apparently unfounded, of negotiations for a $50-million railroad loan in April 1928 (cables, March 19, April 16, and April 27, 1928, from Dewey to the Federal Reserve, *ibid.*).

external municipal loan, the Government will consult the Adviser. . . ." [95] Nevertheless, the borrowing was hardly likely to assist the already weak stabilization bonds.

Poland's trade balance again turned unfavorable and concern over domestic alarm at this unfavorable balance was the reason advanced for requesting an extension of the central bank credit in September 1928. Dewey's grasp of the relationships of the various parties is, perhaps, indicated by the fact that he addressed his first correspondence on the subject to the Bank of France. This may also indicate that the initial role of the Bank of France was not as secondary as the official record might lead one to think. Dewey wrote that the Council of the Bank of Poland had decided, while he was on vacation in August, that:

> . . . while the condition of the Bank required no outside assistance yet owing to the continued unfavorable balance of trade and the fact that the citizens of Poland were becoming somewhat alarmed, for psychological reasons it might be advisable to consider asking for a renewal or extension.
> I am informed that you have represented the 14 participating banks in the existing credit and for this reason I am writing you directly with the request that Governors Montagu Norman and Benj. Strong be communicated with at as early a date as possible with the view of ascertaining their reaction to the suggestion of the Bank of Poland.[96]

The Bank of France replied, of course, that the Federal Reserve Bank had taken the initiative in the original credit and that the interest of the Bank of France was simply that of a participant. A request was then addressed to the Federal Reserve and the credit was, with some reluctance, renewed for another year. But the fact that it was considered necessary to renew it, at the cost of another commission charge, scarcely indicated that Poland was in a strong financial position.

Thus, the fact that Dewey experienced no difficulties in his position as Adviser does not necessarily indicate that his powers were adequate under the plan, much less that events proved that control was unnecessary. Before the event, the question as to whether or not

[95] Plan of Stabilization in J. F. Dulles, *Poland*, p. 15.

[96] Letter, September 5, 1928, Dewey to Moreau, Federal Reserve, Correspondence, Poland, Stabilization, Bank Polski, August 1928.

controls were required was even more open to doubt. The Poles
stressed that they had no external treaty obligations as had Germany, Austria, and Hungary; that no foreign governments were
guaranteeing their loan as had been the case with Austria; and that,
contrary to Austria and Hungary, which had been in desperate condition at the time of the loan, Poland had been stabilized *de facto*
for a considerable period.[97] None of these arguments, however,
sound very convincing, at least to me. Poland did have external
treaty obligations, although admittedly badly defined, and her foreign relations were far less secure than those of Austria and Hungary. No foreign governments were guaranteeing her loan, but the
extension of a central bank credit came close to being a moral guarantee. She had stabilized *de facto* but on the basis of an unusual
grouping of favorable circumstances and after a considerable period
of extreme inflationary experience. In addition, internal political
conditions were not such as to inspire great confidence, her administrative officials were inexperienced and inclined to irresponsible action, and—perhaps most significantly—her credit standing abroad
was extremely weak. Thus, there was considerable justification for
the views of Norman and Schacht.

The compromise arrived at with respect to control combined the
worst features of both views. It was a control which was so weakened
as to border on being no control at all. Yet, it was designed to leave
the impression, particularly among the investing public, that it was
adequate to warrant an improvement in Poland's credit standing.
From the point of view of central bank cooperation, arriving at the
compromise involved a heavy strain on the available supply of good
will. It was an illogical compromise because, if control was necessary
at all, it was the substance, not the shadow, of control which was
needed. But it was the shadow which the plan provided.

Even more serious from the standpoint of central bank cooperation was the behavior of the authorities of the time of the Federal
Reserve Bank of New York. They succeeded in establishing the
bank as the leader of the consortium of central banks and then re-

97 "Form and Purpose of Control," enclosed with letter, March 30, 1927, Pierre
Denis to Harrison, Federal Reserve, Correspondence, Poland, Stabilization, Bank
Polski, April 1926–August 1927.

fused to accept the responsibilities of that position. Worse yet, they pressed Norman and Schacht into the very positions which both had unequivocally stated they did not want to take. Norman and Schacht had made it abundantly clear that they were willing to participate on the basis of accepting the judgment of the Federal Reserve Bank of New York as to the soundness of the program, but they did not want to share the responsibility by passing upon the program itself. This was a perfectly understandable point of view and one which had been established by precedent in like cases. In the Belgian case, the other central banks had accepted the judgment of the Bank of England and the Federal Reserve Bank and participated on that basis. In the Italian case, which immediately followed the Polish, the Federal Reserve authorities raised no objection when the other central banks were specifically asked in advance if they would accept the judgments of Norman and Strong. The way in which the Polish matter was put to Norman and Schacht, after they had made their stand clear, was almost immoral. In effect, the Federal Reserve Bank of New York said: "We do not want you to participate unless you yourself are satisfied with the plan, but if you do not participate you understand that we central bankers all agree that this is an indication that you are not interested in cooperating with other banks of issue."

The Federal Reserve authorities, and particularly those of the Board in Washington, were concerned, of course, about the political reaction in the United States if they appeared to be taking a leading role in European political affairs. But the danger of such adverse political reaction was evident from the start. If the Federal Reserve authorities were not prepared to brave that reaction, they should not have put themselves in such a position that it was impossible for any other central bank to take over leadership from them. Not that any other bank wanted the leadership, at least not openly; but the Reserve should not have pre-empted the position unless it was prepared to accept the responsibility. If it had not taken the leadership at the start, there were only two central banks which could have done so. One was the Bank of England, which would certainly have insisted upon a League plan. It is quite possible that Poland would have refused to accept the League; but if there were no other alternative, this is not certain. The other possibility was the Bank of France, which would have welcomed the opportunity and been welcomed by the Poles. The danger here was that the other central banks would not follow the leadership of the Bank of France because of the known French political interests in Poland. It is highly unlikely that Schacht would have joined such an arrangement at least without even more concessions than the Federal Reserve extracted from Poland. If Schacht had not joined, some of the other European central banks might have stayed out. It is just as doubtful that Norman would have joined a Bank of France arrangement at this time and this, certainly, would have kept others out. It is true that Norman eventually joined a Bank of France sponsored plan for Rumania, but in part this was because the precedent of the Polish case existed and in part because there was a reluctance to strain inter-central bank relations any further than they had already been strained. Thus, if the Federal Reserve had not taken leadership, it is quite possible that a central bank credit for Poland could not have been arranged. It is by no means clear that this would have been such a terrible misfortune for Poland. But, even if it had been, it would have been preferable for the world to the ill will and mistrust generated by the way in which the credit arrangement was handled.

Chapter V. RUMANIA

Although the Federal Reserve Bank of New York and the Bank of France collaborated in arranging the Polish stabilization credit, there was no doubt, even on the part of the Federal Reserve Bank, that the Federal Reserve was the principal responsible party. At least formally, the Bank of France was relegated to the quite secondary role of arranging the final details of the credit as agent for the New York bank. The suspicion is strong that the Bank of France actually played a much larger role than this, but there was no formal recognition of it and the Bank of France preferred not to appear as a principal responsible party. In the Rumanian case, the two again collaborated, although the collaboration was rather forced upon the Federal Reserve Bank of New York and was certainly somewhat less than whole-hearted on its part. The Bank of France clearly and openly took the leadership and tried to maneuver the reluctant Federal Reserve into a position of co-responsibility as a means of overcoming resistance on the part of some of the other European central banks.

There were many points of similarity in the postwar situations of Poland and Rumania. Like Poland, Rumania found herself faced at the end of the war with the necessity of integrating widely disparate territories into an economic, political, and social unit.[1] In this task, however, she had the advantage that she was not a newly created nation. The territorial nucleus of the nation existed in prewar Rumania. The problem was one of grafting to this territory various newly

[1] The population of Rumania was more than doubled between 1914 and 1922 largely as a result of territorial acquisitions granted by the Treaty of Trianon (Nicolas Angelesco, *L'Expérience monétaire Roumaine (1914–1927)* [Paris, 1928], p. 148).

acquired regions. She had the nucleus of a trained civil service, though poorly trained and with a tradition of corruption, which had to be expanded but not created afresh. On the other hand, there was much less of a sense of national unity in the enlarged Rumania than there was in reconstituted Poland. In any event, the Rumanian tasks of economic reorientation, of transportation integration, and of monetary unification were very like those of Poland's.

For Rumania, the war did not continue beyond the armistice in 1918. But to some extent its place was taken by latent internal unrest and political instability. Nor was all the unrest latent. A workers' demonstration in Bucharest in 1920 was only dispersed by bloodshed and the unrest was only prevented from breaking out more frequently and more violently by an extensive repressive apparatus under the Minister of the Interior.[2] Throughout most of the 1920s, the internal political situation was uneasily dominated by Marshal Averescu and by Ionel Bratianu of the Liberal Party.[3] The domination depended largely upon the personal strength of these two, and particularly that of Bratianu, and the situation was complicated after the death of King Ferdinand in 1927 by the threat of the return from exile of Prince Carol, a threat that finally materialized in 1930.[4] While the internal unrest and political instability in Rumania did not hinder reconstruction by causing additional destruction of property, it did make the task of attacking reconstruction resolutely more difficult than it otherwise would have been.

If, in modern terminology, post-World War I Poland was in the position of a developing nation, Rumania was in that of a truly underdeveloped nation. She was even more dependent on agriculture than was Poland [5] and it is doubtful whether she had yet reached a stage of economic development that could support an industrialization effort. Yet the Liberal government of Bratianu attempted to force industrialization, while at the same time trying to exclude foreign capital from the process.[6] The result was heavy economic pres-

---

2 Seton-Watson, *Eastern Europe between the Wars 1918–1941*, p. 200.
3 *Ibid.*, pp. 198–206.   4 *Ibid.*, p. 203.
5 Seventy-eight per cent of her population was engaged in agriculture (*ibid.*, p. 75).
6 *Ibid.*, pp. 200–201. Angelesco explains the absence of capital inflows by foreign mistrust of the leu. This alone might have limited the inflow, but there

sure on the peasant population and a persistent capital shortage. The barriers to the entry of foreign investment capital were not removed until the arrival in late 1928 of a National Peasant Party government under Iulius Maniu.[7] Their removal corresponded in time with *de jure* stabilization and the combination of circumstances led to an inflow of foreign capital which at least temporarily eased the burden on the Rumanian peasant.

Rumanian inflation, while considerable, never reached the catastrophic proportions that Poland experienced in 1923. Most of the Rumanian inflation occurred in the immediate postwar years, and by the end of 1922 the leu had fallen to a level of about one-half of a United States cent from its prewar value of 19.3 cents.[8] Thereafter it fluctuated around this value until it was stabilized *de facto* in the spring of 1927 at about 0.6 cents. But, while her inflation had not been as serious as Poland's, this does not mean that Rumania's monetary situation was a great deal sounder than Poland's. A disproportionate amount of the liabilities of the Rumanian National Bank consisted of notes issued for the account of the state.[9] In addition, the Rumanian National Bank was in a highly illiquid condition.[10] As late as February of 1929, Charles Rist was discussing with the executive board of the bank the elimination of such nonliquid items from the bank's portfolio and, in exasperation, finally asked: "mais enfin qu'appelez-vous un effet liquide?" [But then, what do you call a liquid security?] He was told in good faith, "c'est un effet dont les intérêts sont regulièrement payés." [11] [It's a security on which the interest is paid regularly.]

One of the principal reasons for the large percentage of the note circulation that had been issued for account of the state was the operation of unifying the currency that was in use at the end of the war. In addition to the notes of the National Bank of Rumania, the only legal currency, there were large quantities of three other kinds

---

can be no doubt that the Rumanian government placed obstacles in the path of the inflow of foreign investment capital (Angelesco, *L'Expérience monétaire*, pp. 164, 187–89).

7 Seton-Watson, *Eastern Europe between the Wars 1918–1941*, p. 129.

8 Crane, *The Little Entente*, p. 61.

9 Angelesco, *L'Expérience monétaire*, p. 43.   10 *Ibid.*, p. 153.

11 Roger Auboin, *Les Missions de Charles Rist en Roumainie 1929–1932* (Paris, undated), pp. 9–10.

of money in circulation. During the Austro-German occupation, the Central Powers issued leu notes through the Banque Générale Roumaine, which were only valid in the occupied territory. In the newly acquired territories, larger amounts of Austrian crowns and Russian rubles were circulating which had to be replaced by Rumanian lei. The operation of monetary unification was not effected until the end of 1921 and resulted in a 7.5-billion-lei increase in the debt of the state to the National Bank.[12] Upon completion of the operation, however, the government ceased its calls to the National Bank for financial aid,[13] which may account for the uncertain halt in the depreciation of the leu. Note issue continued to expand, nevertheless, under the pressure of commercial and industrial demand. In May 1925 a convention between the National Bank and the Ministry of Finance fixed a maximum limit of 21.071 billion lei for the note circulation.[14] No serious attempt at *de facto,* let alone *de jure,* stabilization was made, however, until 1927.

In the spring of that year, the leu was effectively stabilized, and in October the Rumanians went to Geneva in search of a foreign loan.[15] They were unwilling, however, to accept the conditions that would be demanded if they went through the Financial Committee of the League and began to look elsewhere for help. Already on October 18, 1927, Charles Rist advised Moreau that the Rumanians wanted to stabilize without going through the League and Moreau commented in his diary that perhaps the French could suggest to them that they apply to France and the United States as in the Polish case.[16] On November 23, 1927, Moreau learned that Clément Moret, an official in the French Finance Ministry, had offered Rumania a loan of 1500 million francs under the following conditions:

12 Angelesco, *L'Expérience monétaire,* pp. 34–43.   13 *Ibid.,* p. 149.
14 *Ibid.,* p. 160.
15 Chandler, *Benjamin Strong, Central Banker,* pp. 403–404.
16 Moreau, *Souvenirs,* p. 208. That Moreau considered the League and the Bank of England as one and his aim was to displace the Bank of England is, perhaps, best indicated by his reaction to this opportunity and by an entry of February 6, 1928, in his diary: "Ne conviendrait-il pas d'avoir une conversation sérieuse avec M. Norman, pour essayer de partager l'Europe en deux zones d'influence financière qui seraient attribuées respectivement à la France et à l'Angleterre?" [Would it not be advisable to have a serious conversation with Mr. Norman in order to attempt to divide Europe into two zones of financial influence, one of which would be allocated to France and the other to England?] (*ibid.,* p. 489).

1. Rumania would not go to the Financial Committee of the League of Nations to stabilize the leu.
2. Questions concerning prewar and war debts would be settled.
3. One billion of the loan would be furnished from the United States and 500 million from France. (The basis of the French belief that 1 billion francs—approximately $40 million—could be floated in the United States is not clear.)
4. 250 million of the 1500 million would be spent in France.[17]

From the point of view of this study, the first condition of this offer is particularly pertinent. In actual fact, nothing came of the proposal, but the Bank of England later became convinced that the French government had taken official steps to encourage the Rumanians not to turn to the League of Nations for stabilization assistance. Both the French government and the Bank of France vehemently denied that any such action had been taken. While there may have been some basis for their denial in the form in which the British made the accusation, the fact remains that the denial was made with less than full candor.[18]

In any case, General Antonescu arrived in Paris as a representative of the Rumanian government to continue discussions with the French, and on December 15, 1927, he and Moreau had a long conversation. Moreau told Antonescu that he had thought that the Rumanians only wanted a loan at the moment for purposes of reorganizing their railroad system.[19] Since, however, they had decided to stabilize at the same time, it would be necessary for them to first consult with private bankers in order to discover what they would offer. When this had been done, the Rumanian National Bank could ask the Bank of France to serve as intermediary to arrange a central bank credit. The Bank of France would then send someone to Bucharest to study the situation and, if the results of the study were favorable, would ask for the support of other banks of issue. He advised Antonescu that Rumania would have to submit to controls, but the chosen controller would be French and the Bank of

[17] *Ibid.*, p. 432.
[18] See pp. 125–26. It is inconceivable that Moret, who was Poincaré's principal assistant in the Treasury, made this offer unofficially.
[19] The Bank of England considered that such development objectives were, in fact, the real purpose of the loan (see p. 106), and the ultimate uses to which the loan proceeds were put supports this view.

France would try to keep the controls as painless as possible.[20]

Within three weeks of this conversation, the Rumanian government had invited Jean Monnet as a representative of Blair and Company to visit Bucharest to discuss a stabilization program. It had also invited M. Gaston Jèze, professor of the law faculty in Paris, and an engineer of the Compagnie des Chemins de Fer du Nord to Rumania to study on the spot the condition of public finances and of the Rumanian railroads. In a letter of January 4, 1928, D. M. Burilleanu, Governor of the Rumanian National Bank, advised Moreau of these facts and invited him to send a representative to Bucharest to study the entire situation so that Moreau would be in a position to decide whether the Bank of France would be willing to organize a consortium of central banks to extend a credit to the Rumanian bank.[21] By the middle of January, Pierre Quesnay had left for Rumania.

Until this time, however, the Rumanians had apparently not entirely discarded the possibility that they might have to go through the League in order to effect legal stabilization. M. Oscar Kiriacescu, Deputy Governor of the Bank of Rumania, had been expected to visit the Bank of England in early January 1928 in order to discuss stabilization with League support. The visit did not take place, however, and on January 21 Norman wired Strong to advise him of that fact and to ask him to discuss the situation with Sir Otto Niemeyer of the Bank of England, who was then on his way to New York. Norman's wire went on to say:

> Roumanian Government appear to have abandoned idea of stabilization through League and are proceeding to negotiate with French Banks and Blairs. Indeed Monnet and French experts are in Roumania and Quesnay goes immediately.
>
> Support of League appears particularly needful in case of Roumania because of disturbed internal conditions and because of unsettled external matters, e.g., Hungarian complaints, pre-war Bonds, German claims. I am advising you in the hope that Polish case may not be made a precedent for Central Bank Credit based on negotiations of Private Bankers.[22]

20 Moreau, *Souvenirs,* p. 452.

21 Letter, January 4, 1928, Burilleanu to Moreau, Federal Reserve, Correspondence, Rumania, January 1928–.

22 Cable, January 21, 1928, Norman to Strong, *ibid.* Norman saw the danger to European financial unity which threatened. In a letter of January 24, 1928, to

The Polish precedent and the rise of the Bank of France to a position of power opened up the possibility for the debtor countries to exploit differing national interests. In a short note written about this time, Niemeyer pointed out:

The Roumanians for a considerable time have been trying to induce various so-called experts to express either orally or in writing opinions about their financial position which could be used for market purposes. They tried very hard in the first place to get Salter to express such an opinion. They also tried to get me to express such an opinion. They have now apparently turned to the French, no doubt in the hopes that Monsieur Quesney's [*sic*] reputation will be useful to them. I think it is a pity that Mr. Moreau let himself be inveigled into this position as I am quite certain that he will not be allowed to get a really complete and thorough review of the position in this way. The presence of the Chief Engineer of the Nord Railway shows what the real object is.[23]

In a note reporting on conversations he had had in Paris on January 18, 1928, Siepmann pointed out that the Rumanians had expressly quoted the Polish precedent in support of their avoidance of the League. Even in the Polish case, Siepmann had been strongly against a non-League plan, but his note goes on to underline the differences in the Polish and Rumanian situations and to stress the dangers in the current overtures:

The Roumanian problem is essentially different from that of Poland. It is to *restore* the credit which Roumania once enjoyed and has now forfeited. This means that action must be taken internally and spontaneously, *before* external help can be of any avail. The party feud has to be composed and a national policy adopted which gives some prospect of social and political stability; and in the second place, tangible evidence has to be given of willingness to abandon the traditional policy of the Liberal Party towards external commitments and obligations; in other words, outstanding disputes, financial and political, with other countries have to be settled instead of being left for ever in suspense. Both these things require to be done by the

---

Strong, he wrote: "I am disappointed at the way in which these affairs seem to be tending, not only because the support of the Financial Committee of the League is likely to be avoided but also because financially, if not politically, Europe seems to be splitting up into groups" (*ibid.*).

[23] Niemeyer memorandum forwarded to New York by letter, January 24, 1928, Norman to Strong, *ibid.*

Roumanians themselves, if there is to be any sure basis for the grant of further external help. To engage in discussions, before these things have been done, about the form which such external help might take is to encourage the illusion that it may not be necessary after all to make a settlement, internally and externally, of the past; and the longer this illusion is maintained, the longer such a settlement is likely to be postponed.[24]

The Federal Reserve Bank of New York, influenced perhaps by some of its difficulties in the recent Polish experience, leaned at this time toward the Bank of England attitude toward Rumanian stabilization. On January 23, 1928, Moreau wrote to Strong to advise him of the approach of the Rumanians and of Quesnay's mission in Bucharest. His letter indicated that it was his intention, if he felt justified in supporting the Rumanian request, to proceed as had Strong in the Polish precedent and as had the Bank of England in the Italian precedent. But he wrote that he expected to ask the New York Bank to study the situation with him to decide if the two could approach the other banks of issue jointly.[25] After discussing the matter with Strong, who was absent from the bank because of illness, Harrison replied on February 3, 1928. His letter indicated a polite interest, but went on to say:

In fact, we know very little about the situation and at this distance, and with so little information available, it is difficult for us to study it. For that reason, we shall be especially interested to know what Mr. Quesnay is able to ascertain. It has been our impression, however, that conditions in Roumania—financial, economic and political may be so confused and uncertain as to prompt the question whether they are susceptible to satisfactory solution by a program such as the Polish one, to which you refer; or whether, indeed, they might not require a more emphatic investigation and control under League auspices.[26]

Upon Quesnay's return from Bucharest, Moreau hastened to arrange for him to visit New York in order to present his findings in

24 Siepmann Note of Conversations held in Paris on January 18, 1928, forwarded by Norman's letter of January 24, 1928, *ibid.*

25 Letter, January 23, 1928, Moreau to Strong, *ibid.*

26 Letter, February 3, 1928, Harrison to Moreau, *ibid.* Upon his arrival in New York, Niemeyer cabled Norman on February 2, 1928, that ". . . I find no predisposition here to credit for Roumania which is not regarded as comparable to Poland" *ibid.*

person. Since Strong had been planning to sail for Europe in the near future, plans were made for Quesnay to rush to New York so as to see Strong before his departure. Strong's sailing was deferred, however, and on February 16, 1928, Strong sent Moreau a cable that made the position of the Federal Reserve Bank more specific:

It occurs to me after talking with Niemeyer that since Roumanian stabilization is not a matter in which we can properly take the initiative, it would be helpful to us in considering whether we shall participate to have assurances before talking with Quesnay that other leading Central Banks are in agreement as to the handling of the problem and are prepared to cooperate. Since my sailing has been deferred and there is no need for hastening Quesnay's visit on that account, I should be grateful for some further word from you.[27]

It was at this point that serious misunderstandings began to develop, and this time it was the Federal Reserve Bank of New York that found itself being pushed into a position it had specifically rejected. The Rumanian National Bank formally requested the Bank of France to take the necessary steps to obtain the assistance of other banks of issue in a Rumanian stabilization effort. Moreau and Quesnay visited the Bank of England on February 22, 1928, to press for British cooperation in a central bank credit for Rumania organized under the sponsorship of the Bank of France. Incidentally, it was at this time that the Bank of France also asserted its claim to having been treated as an inferior in the past and its refusal to be so treated in the future.[28] It is quite possible that Moreau sincerely felt slighted by the treatment which the Bank of France had received in the course of previous stabilization negotiations, particularly in the Belgian case; but the timing of the claim to equal treatment was certainly useful in pressing Rumanian stabilization. That this factor played a large part in Moreau's decision to demand equality of treatment at this time and that more than injured personal feelings were involved is indicated by an entry in Moreau's diary on February 28, 1928, that "nous sommes engagés dans une lutte très serrée avec la Banque d'Angleterre, d'une portée politique considérable, car il s'agit moins d'une rivalité d'influence entre la

[27] Cable, February 16, 1928, Strong to Moreau, *ibid.*
[28] Moreau, *Souvenirs,* pp. 505–507.

Banque d'Angleterre et la Banque de France que de savoir si l'influence anglaise remplacera dans les États de la Petite Entente l'influence française." [29] [We are engaged in a very bitter struggle, and one of considerable political significance, with the Bank of England. This is less a question of rivalry for influence between the Bank of England and the Bank of France than it is one of ascertaining whether British influence shall replace French within the Little Entente.]

Unfortunately, Norman was ill the day of Moreau's visit and the discussions were held with Cecil Lubbock, Deputy Governor of the Bank of England.[30] From the correspondence record, Lubbock appears to have been extremely insecure in his position, as perhaps anyone working in the shadow of Montagu Norman was bound to be.[31] In any case, his cables and letters are filled with claims of his incapacity, except for his extreme devotion to Norman, for fulfilling the duties of his position. One has the impression of a definite lack of force, and certainly he was not Norman's equal in such delicate negotiations as these. It is to be doubted whether Moreau would have been able to present his claims to equal treatment with the same force or to leave with the feeling that he had overwhelmed the British [32] if Norman had been his protagonist. As it was, Moreau extracted a promise of Bank of England cooperation in a program that the Bank of France would prepare in agreement with the Fed-

29 *Ibid.*, p. 507.

30 Clay, *Lord Norman*, pp. 260–61. Moreau and others had the feeling that Norman's illness may have been more diplomatic than real. Dr. Stewart, formerly of the Federal Reserve Board and at this time a special employee of the Bank of England, positively assured Strong, who had absolute confidence in Stewart's integrity, that Norman's illness was very real and not diplomatic (Strong's memorandum re: Bank of England–Bank of France Relations, Paris, May 24, 1928, Strong Papers, European Trips, 1928).

31 Both Clay and Einzig comment upon an element in Norman's character that made it extremely difficult to work closely with him. Clay uses the expression "prima donna" and Einzig the term "despot." But the despotism was of a subtle and complex type. Both biographers agree that it was not based upon tactics calculated to inspire fear, but rather a strength of character which made it difficult to oppose his will. Einzig cites the case of a Director of the Bank of England who told Einzig of an occasion when he went to a meeting of the Court of the bank determined to oppose Norman on a particular matter. In Norman's presence, his determination vanished. Later he was furious with himself, but on the next occasion, the same thing happened (Clay, *Lord Norman*, pp. 482–84, Paul Einzig, *Montagu Norman* [London, 1932], pp. 29–30).

32 Moreau, *Souvenirs*, p. 506.

eral Reserve Bank of New York. Whether this was really the precise form of the agreement reached and just what it meant is not, however, absolutely clear.

Lubbock cabled Strong on February 23 as follows:

Yesterday in the absence of Governor I had conversation with Moreau and Quesnay about Roumania.

Quoting Italian precedent Moreau asked whether we would reciprocate endorsing any arrangements which may be agreed between you and him. Presuming that you would get situation examined with Roumanians at least as rigorously as with Italians we agreed to follow your joint lead since question was put to us explicitly as a test of our sincerity in cooperation and reciprocity.

Roumanian case appears to us to differ from Italian not merely in degree but in kind. Differs incidentally because prior to settlement [settlement] various international obligations obviously necessary; because private bankers interested in obtaining Central Bank Hall marks for their loans; also because money required not entirely for stabilization.

As you know we hold strongly that Roumania is a case for the League and that no other body could frame a scheme commanding general confidence or impose necessary control.[33]

All three of the elements in the Rumanian situation which Lubbock questioned had also been present in the Polish case, but to a lesser degree. Poland also had had outstanding unsettled international obligations at the time of the credit negotiations. In her case, however, the obligations were all of a political nature, arising out of the postwar network of treaties. Being a new nation, her debt burden, both internal and external, was extremely small. Rumania also had her obligations arising out of the postwar political settlement. In addition to these, however, she also had a number of outstanding foreign bond issues on which she had defaulted and it was this aspect of her failure to deal with her international obligations which was to be a major problem in the negotiations.

Part of the proceeds of the Polish stabilization loan was frankly destined for developmental purposes as was the case with the proposed Rumanian loan. The proportion of the loan intended for

[33] Cable, February 23, 1928, Lubbock to Strong, Federal Reserve, Correspondence, Roumania, January 1928–.

such non-monetary purposes was, however, much smaller in the case of Poland than it was in the case of Rumania. In addition, the distribution of the Polish loan proceeds was based upon the Kemmerer recommendations. Despite reservations in some quarters about the Kemmerer mission, there is no doubt that its study of the Polish situation was much more thorough than anything which had been undertaken in Rumania.

The most interesting issue raised by Lubbock was the accusation that private bankers wanted the central bank credit as a seal of approval for the private loan. This element was also present in the Polish loan—and, to a degree, even in the Belgian loan. It was almost inevitable that such support for the private loan would be sought once the principle of combining a central bank credit with a private stabilization loan was established. Since the central bank credit would assuredly be used for this purpose, the significant point is the attitude taken by the major central banks toward their responsibilities in this regard. It has already been brought out that the authorities of the Bank of England considered that, for this reason, a central bank credit should be extended only under such conditions as would justify their own confidence in the safety of the loan. Weak as controls were in the Polish case, they were legally adequate to insure service of the loan. The authorities of the Federal Reserve Bank of New York in the 1920s, on the other hand, adopted the view that, while it was unfortunate that private bankers would use the central bank credit to support their loan issue, this was not a factor to be considered in deciding whether or not to extend the credit.[34]

Lubbock's cable implied that the commitment of the Bank of England was contingent upon joint leadership by the Bank of France and the Federal Reserve Bank of New York. Moreau's diary indicates an understanding that the Bank of England had agreed not to make any special efforts in any way with respect to Rumanian stabilization and to support a program prepared by the Bank of France in agreement with Strong. Whether he understood that this implied joint leadership with the Federal Reserve is not clear from his diary.[35] His cable to Strong implied nothing of the sort: "I have

[34] See p. 121.   [35] Moreau, *Souvenirs,* p. 506.

gone personally to London Wednesday to consider whole situation with Bank of England and distinctly state Rumanian question. I am authorized to assert that Bank of England will conform their attitude to that of Bank of France in Italian matter; they have promised their assistance if I accept to organise cooperation which I shall do only after having your reaction Rumanian programme." [36]

On the other hand, Dr. Walter W. Stewart, formerly of the Federal Reserve and at this time a special employee of the Bank of England, was of the opinion that no definite agreement as to Bank of England participation in the credit had been reached. In his view, the point emphasized by Moreau and accepted by Lubbock was that the Bank of England would refrain from approaching any parties; that is, the Federal Reserve Bank, the Bank of Italy, the Reichsbank or anyone else, with efforts to defeat a French program for Rumania until after representatives of the Bank of France had met with the Federal Reserve. [37]

Whatever may have been the precise agreement reached, Norman, on his return to the bank the next day, immediately wrote a letter of interpretation which made clear that the British commitment was contingent upon Federal Reserve participation as an original and responsible party. Even this was further than he really wanted to go. Lubbock wrote:

Mont was gravely displeased that I should have given any kind of undertaking to Moreau that we would even look at any scheme but a League scheme: he seemed to think that the whole policy that he has been pursuing for the past year or more has been upset: that it is more than likely that eventually you will take up Roumania as you did Poland, and will invite us to come in; and that he might have to go back on everything he has been saying during the last year or two.

I replied that you also are of the opinion that it is probably a case for the League, and that you do not intend to take any initiative or leadership: that if Moreau realizes that you two are in favour of League treatment it would be even easier for Mont to insist on his point of view.

Moreau thinks that hitherto we have been leaving him out in the cold: he claims from henceforth to be treated as an equal: and perhaps I may

[36] Cable, February 24, 1928, Moreau to Strong, Federal Reserve, Correspondence, Roumania, January 1928–.
[37] Strong's Memorandum re: Bank of England–Bank of France Relations, Paris, May 24, 1928, Strong Papers, European Trips, 1928.

have gone too far in what I said in my desire not absolutely to reflect what he put forward as a test of our desire to work in co-operation with him.

Mont says I have put you in an unfair position: that I have left, as it were to your arbitration, a question which he regards as one of principle; in other words, he says that we have left it to *you* to decide whether or not *we* are to come into a *non*-League scheme.

The Roumanian case is so complicated and so full of European politics that I cannot believe that there is any possibility of your taking up Roumania as you took up Poland. If I am right, and if you can help to shepherd Morgan towards the League, we shall have avoided quarrelling with him at this stage, and all may work out happily towards the desired end.[38]

Strong replied to Lubbock's cable on February 24, 1928, sending a copy of his reply to Moreau. After pointing out that the Federal Reserve Bank had not yet had an opportunity to discuss the Rumanian matter with the Bank of France and that its views might change as a result of such discussions, he outlined his present views. Following the usual central banker's ritual in the 1920s, he asserted that New York considered central bank cooperation more important than any particular transaction and expressed the hope that the important European central banks would agree as to whether a League plan or the Italian precedent was preferable in this case. He indicated that the Federal Reserve would predicate its decision on a thorough examination of the entire situation and said:

We have already intimated to Moreau that anticipating the need for somewhat more effective supervision than in certain other cases we might find difficulty in joining a private plan with such responsibilities implied and the circumstances might therefore suggest favouring the League.

We also feel unable to take any initiative or leadership in a situation so remote from our own interests and experience and hope a satisfactory agreement as to the type of plan can first be made by the European central banks.[39]

It is important to note that this was the first indication to the Bank of England of a clearly stated desire on the part of the Federal Reserve Bank of New York to avoid any responsibility or leadership in

[38] Letter, February 28, 1928, Lubbock to Strong, Strong Papers, Bank of England.

[39] Cable, February 24, 1928, Strong to Lubbock (copy to Moreau), Federal Reserve, Correspondence, Roumania, January 1928–.

the Rumanian situation, and it was given after Lubbock and Norman had committed themselves to the Bank of France.

One has the impression, however, that there was more to Strong's declining to accept any form of responsibility than the remoteness of Rumania from Federal Reserve interests and experience. There is a strong feeling that he had no inclination to repeat the harrowing Polish experience. It is quite probable—although my research has revealed no concrete evidence on this score—that he was under some pressure from the Federal Reserve Board as well to avoid anything but a passive role with respect to Rumania. Certainly, the Board could not be expected to welcome the prospect of having to defend before the Administration a second major involvement of the System in Eastern European affairs.

Moreau had suggested to Strong that Quesnay and Kiriacescu come to New York to discuss the entire Rumanian situation. Strong, however, cabled Moreau that, since the Federal Reserve felt unable to take initiative or leadership in the matter, meetings held in New York with a representative of the Rumanian National Bank might be misunderstood; consequently, Rist and Quesnay made the trip alone.[40] After discussions with them, the Federal Reserve Bank of New York had, by March 23, 1928, just about decided to recommend its own participation in the Bank of France sponsored plan. But there was evidently a feeling that such a move might be misunderstood by the Bank of England, and a cable exchange with the Bank of England indicated that there was a subtle difference in interpretation of the move. Strong cabled to Lubbock, with a copy going to Moreau, that

our conversations with Rist and Quesnay have developed the following
  1. Bank of France has substantially concluded agreement upon a program of stabilization prepared by the Roumanians which they believe to be quite satisfactory though they say it may require some further consideration as to detail before they and Roumania and private Bankers are in final agreement
  2. They have been formally requested by Roumanian National Bank to invite other Banks of Issue to participate in a Central Bank credit
  3. Having as you know communicated with us some weeks ago they are now prepared formally to invite Federal Reserve Bank to participate

[40] Cable, February 27, 1928, Strong to Moreau, *ibid.*

in such a Central Bank credit subject to negotiation of the program being satisfactorily concluded and they desire some indication of our probable attitude

4. They will then confirm categorically their advice already given to us
   (a) that Roumania has definitely decided to stabilize without going through the Financial Committee of the League
   (b) that Bank of France is prepared to assume responsibility of leadership without Federal Reserve Bank assuming initiative or joint leadership in preparing or launching plan
   (c) that they are prepared to invite the other banks of issue to join as in other similar cases and desire their co-operation and participation
   (d) that you have also been approached by Bank of France but that some difference of view exists as to interpretation of your reply

5. We are advising you at once in advance of a formal invitation being sent us so that there may be no lack of opportunity to consider every aspect of situation such as would have been afforded by our meeting together

6. As to our own position we feel as already explained
   (a) that the benefits of co-operation are superior to other considerations
   (b) that Roumania is the one to decide for or against one or other method or plan
   (c) that while we have indicated that this might be a suitable opportunity for a League program we could not insist upon it nor attempt to force a decision one way or another by Roumania
   (d) that we would not assume initiative or joint leadership

7. It therefore seems necessary for us now to advise our friends whether we will or will not consider their proposal sympathetically if it is submitted to us

8. Any decision by us at this stage could only go so far as to recommend participation if invited as final decision must be made by the usual procedure

9. But we now see no logical or consistent reason for our declining to so recommend and at the same time we see definite advantages for harmonious co-operation by our extending to the Bank of France exactly the same support for a plan under their leadership that they and other Banks of Issue have given under the leadership of other Central Banks

10. So if there are any further facts for us to consider I hope you will cable me fully with whatever expression of your views and attitude you feel desirable.[41]

41 Cable, March 23, 1928, Strong to Lubbock (copy to Moreau), *ibid.*

At the same time, however, Strong and Harrison sent a private cable to Lubbock, which was not shown to the French:

This very private cable is necessary to a full understanding of our #75 and we hope will clear up any possibility of misjudging our position. Our friends have not seen it.

Matters seem to have developed so that we may appear to you to be between two contending parties and thus may be embarrassed by whatever decision we make.

This might have been the case had there been anything in our communications to London or Paris oral or written which would have permitted such a situation to arise or have made decisions by others in any way dependent upon ours

Having pointed out that we would not accept responsibility for a Roumanian programme and having reserved complete freedom of action regardless of what program might be or by whom proposed it now seems necessary for us to decide upon that basis whether we shall participate in a credit at the invitation of the Bank of France. This course can cause us no embarrassment so long as we are violating no understanding express or implied

Should our decision lead you to assume that we have sufficient familiarity with the plan to satisfy you, we would then be assuming the very responsibility of leadership or initiation which we have disclaimed from the start

We shall of course reply to the Bank of France just as we would have replied to you had you initiated a plan for Roumania or had a league plan been submitted to us through you. This we believe is the best way to express our conviction of the importance of Central Bank co-operation

We hope therefore to hear fully and frankly from you in reply to our #75 in which we have endeavoured to express the situation fairly before any commitments are made

Finally and privately we wish to be certain that you and Norman realize

(a) that we are not a bit embarrassed
(b) that we are rooting for Central Bank co-operation and
(c) that we still love you [42]

Lubbock replied in kind with two cables, one of which was intended to be seen by the French, the other strictly private. In the quotation below, the private cable has been inserted paragraph by paragraph in parentheses in the open cable.

[42] Cable, March 23, 1928, Strong and Harrison to Lubbock, *ibid.*

1. Naturally we regard Central Bank co-operation as a primary interest (But we feel that co-operation can not rightly be invoked to commit all other Central Banks to action based upon the sole responsibility and recommendations of one among them)

2. That is why we accepted Italian procedure for Roumania, though circumstances differ materially (By Italian procedure we mean that if you and our friends examine, approve and recommend a plan, we will come in on your joint authority as they did in ours)

3. We do not claim initiative or leadership and should be content to co-operate in any plan similarly approved (In view of exceptional difficulties of [sic] we feel that any plan must be rigorously examined before it can qualify as approved)

4. We still believe in League solution but agree that it may be difficult in present circumtsances (This and the unsettled state of the country may be a reason for delay rather than for haste. We are not alone in thinking that the present moment may not be quite opportune)

5. As you do not assume joint leadership and responsibility for the plan we could not participate without further examination and endorsement (Other Central banks would doubtless look to us for guidance and we cannot participate in a plan which we should not be satisfied to recommend)

6. We wonder whether Central banks credit is technically necessary in addition to the loan. We have been discouraging the fashion and have in mind pending cases such as Greece and Jugoslavia [43] (Is there not some risk that the names and authority of Central banks may be enlisted on insufficient evidence to assist the marketing of bonds by private houses)

7. Our best regards to Rist and Quesnay (But we are disturbed about possible consequences of their thinking that co-operation is at stake and we thank you for paragraph 8 of your #76) [44]

[43] Neither Greek nor Yugoslav stabilization involved a credit extension by a consortium of central banks. Greece received a stabilization and refugee loan in January 1928 through the League of Nations (League of Nations, *Reconstruction Schemes in the Inter-War Period*, pp. 168–69). Yugoslavia negotiated with the Bank of England and with the League, and a stabilization plan was prepared in 1928 with the advice of H. A. Siepmann. The negotiations were broken off, however, and *de jure* stabilization was not effected until 1931. It was then carried out under French auspices and with a French loan (cable, June 16, 1928, Harrison to Case, Harrison Collection, Binder 34). See also Brown, *The International Gold Standard*, pp. 919–21; Moreau, *Souvenirs*, pp. 536–37; Margaret G. Myers, *Paris as a Financial Centre* (New York, 1936), p. 85.

[44] Cables, March 23, 1928, Lubbock to Strong and Harrison, Federal Reserve, Correspondence, Roumania, January 1928–. In a letter of March 29, 1928, Lubbock again tried to make clear the Bank of England understanding of the Italian precedent, saying: "I will only say that I trust that you agree with our interpretation of the 'Italian precedent' viz: that it implies leadership and re-

There are several interesting points in these cables of Lubbock's. First, there is the idea that cooperation among central banks in extending credits should be based upon joint responsibility and recommendation of at least two among them. This was a new concept and it is questionable whether it could be supported by precedent. While the Federal Reserve and the Bank of France collaborated in the Polish program, one must strain the meaning of words to assert that they assumed joint responsibility. In fact, it has been argued here that one of the defects of that program was that no major central bank admitted responsibility for it. Second, Lubbock's cables clearly indicate the attitude of the Bank of England with respect to its responsibilities, not only to the market, but to the smaller central banks as well. Third, it questions the whole idea of combining a central bank credit with a market loan. After Rumania, the practice did in fact fall into disfavor until the difficulties of the summer of 1931, when joint central bank credits were again extended. But they were still not tied to a private bankers' loan. One has the impression, however, that all these arguments were marshaled to support a fundamental distaste for the transaction based upon mistrust of the Rumanian situation and of the Bank of France.

In any event, the formal invitation from the Bank of France to the Federal Reserve Bank of New York specifically stated that the Bank of France would assume the responsibility and initiative for the credit without the Federal Reserve assuming a joint responsibility with them.[45] On this basis, Strong agreed, subject to the approval of the Federal Reserve Board, to participate up to a maximum of $10 million; but he made clear to Rist that he did not want the Bank of France to use his influence in order to obtain the agreement of other banks.[46]

Even before the formal invitation from the Bank of France to participate in the credit was received by the Federal Reserve Bank of New York, however, the question of the political propriety of Federal Reserve participation arose. On March 21, 1928, the *United*

---

sponsibility on your part, and not merely the acceptance by you of an invitation to participate in a credit" (Strong Papers, Bank of England).

[45] Letter, March 28, 1928, Rist to Strong, Federal Reserve, Correspondence, Roumania, January 1928–.

[46] Moreau, *Souvenirs*, pp. 531–32.

States Daily, a New York newspaper, published a letter of Congress-
man Emanuel Celler of Brooklyn to the Secretary of State, which
called upon the State Department to forbid any stabilization or
other loan to Rumania because of alleged Rumanian treaty viola-
tions as a result of her persecution of Rumanian Jews. Strong and
Harrison became concerned as to whether or not the State Department would regard a protest of this sort of sufficient consequence to
justify their expressing a view with respect to loans to Rumania and
whether Federal Reserve participation in a credit might be embar-
rassing to the State Department. In addition, Strong was concerned
about whether ". . . political conditions in Roumania are such that
any loan or credit at this time might be so hopelessly involved in
party controversy as to make the granting or withholding of the
loan the subject of some political upheaval." [47]

Apart from the anti-Semitic riots at this time, the political situation in Rumania was extremely uncertain as a result of the recent
death of both King Ferdinand and Ionel Bratianu. A regency was established to govern for Carol's four-year-old son, Mihai, and Ionel's
brother, Vintila Bratianu, took over the leadership of the Liberal
Party. But the government was very insecure and finally fell to the
National Peasant Party under Dr. Iulius Maniu in November
1928.[48] The Liberal Party's foreign orientation was French and the
United States Minister in Bucharest felt that it sought to strengthen
its internal position through the stabilization loan. The National
Peasant Party's foreign orientation leaned more toward England,
Germany, and the United States. At this time it had stated publicly
that it would not repudiate foreign financial obligations contracted
by the Liberals should it come to power,[49] although in the summer
of 1928 it announced that it would not consider itself bound by a
contract for a stabilization loan ratified by a Parliament elected by
fraud and violence (i.e., contracted by the Bratianu government).[50]
Thus, the Rumanian internal political situation was scarcely pro-

[47] Letter, March 26, 1928, Strong to Harrison, Federal Reserve, Correspondence, Roumania, January 1928–.
[48] Crane, *The Little Entente,* pp. 65–67.
[49] Letter, March 5, 1928, United States Minister at Bucharest to the Secretary
of State, Federal Reserve, Correspondence, Roumania, January 1928–.
[50] Crane, *The Little Entente,* p. 67.

pitious for the extension of a credit to the National Bank, let alone
the flotation of a long-term loan.

Harrison discussed the situation with the United States Department of State, making clear that the Federal Reserve was not asking
for State Department approval, since the Reserve did not consider
this necessary and felt that the State Department did not want
to be put in the position of approving or disapproving specific Federal Reserve transactions. They were interested in knowing, however, whether, in the opinion of the Department, political conditions in Rumania were such that the granting or withholding of a
loan or credit might be a serious political question and whether the
Department might be embarrassed if the Federal Reserve extended
a credit. He was advised that the Department saw no reason not to
go ahead but that it considered that "Roumania at the moment is
perhaps the most unstable politically of all the Balkan States." [51]
At this point, Harrison adopted a very peculiar point of view:

I then told him that in a monetary and economic sense Rumania appeared
to be as susceptible to monetary stabilization at this time as most of the
other countries which had undertaken de jure stabilization, that inasmuch
as that was so the Federal Reserve Bank of New York felt that it would be
much more 'political' for the New York bank to refuse the invitation to
participate in the credit because of the fact that the only substantial
ground which we could give for such a refusal was political.[52]

It is not clear in what sense Harrison meant the term "political."
It is possible that he was thinking in terms of the internal political
reaction in the United States. But he must also have had in mind
the internal political situation in Rumania and international political considerations. In so far as favoring one political party or the
other within Rumania, either granting the credit or withholding it
was to support one political party or the other. In this sense, taking
sides was unavoidable. More significantly, however, there was the
question of Rumanian political stability. If there was likely to be serious unrest in Rumania, or if a new government might repudiate

---

[51] Memorandum to the Confidential Files, March 28, 1928, subject: "Roumania," Federal Reserve, Correspondence, Roumania, January 1928–.
[52] Memorandum to the Confidential Files, April 6, 1928, subject: "Roumania,"
ibid.

the foreign obligations of its predecessor, the granting of a credit was scarcely good business. Even if the credit, granted as it was to the National Bank rather than to the government, was secure, there remained the safety of the loan. The Department raised this question by asking whether the New York bank had considered that granting a credit ". . . would be used as an argument by bond salesmen, that the Federal Reserve bank had approved of the issue of the loan in America." [53] Harrison's answer is in sharp contrast to the attitude of the Bank of England on this point:

I told him that it was no doubt true that in all transactions of this kind, in the Belgian case and in the Polish case as well as in the proposed Rumanian case, a credit by banks of issue made a talking point for bond salesmen and that respective bond buyers took it into consideration making up their minds about purchases, but I said that I regarded that as an unfortunate incident to the business which we felt it was necessary for us to do as a bank of issue in our efforts to promote stabilization abroad.[54]

This is indeed a peculiar line of thought. Harrison considered it necessary for a bank of issue to undertake such business as these credit extensions for the purpose of promoting stabilization abroad. One can scarcely quarrel with this point of view, but he then goes on to say that it was no concern of the Federal Reserve, or presumably of any other central bank in his opinion, whether or not the related private bond issue was sound. Not only did his attitude ignore the central bank's inescapable responsibility to the market, it ran the risk of resulting in the failure to accomplish the very purpose for which the credit was extended. If the central bankers wished to promote stabilization, they had to assure themselves of the soundness of a stabilization loan before lending it their support. After all, the loan and the credit were both part of a single program, and if any part of that program was unsound the entire program

[53] *Ibid.*
[54] *Ibid.* The Bank of England was not alone in feeling that the central banks had to guard against their names being used to support weak bond issues. Strong, after a discussion with Schacht, wrote: "One of Schacht' [sic] chief objections to this business [the Roumanian], as well as the Polish, was the fact that the bankers were put in a position to trade too definitely on the value of the support of the banks of issue. I guess he is right" (letter, July 13, 1928, Strong to Harrison, Strong Papers, European Trips, 1928).

was likely to fail. In particular, Rumanian stabilization was designed in part to stimulate a flow of private capital to Rumania. Any threat of default on the stabilization loan would hardly encourage further capital inflow and, without this, stabilization was threatened.

Between the end of April and the end of May 1928, Moreau visited the Bank of England, the Reichsbank, and the Bank of Italy and secured what he took to be their agreement to participate.[55] It is doubtful, however, that the commitments were as unconditional as he apparently took them to be. As late as July 11, 1928, Strong commented: "You will doubtless notice in the papers issued by Governor Moreau some pretty definite statements as to the approval by the Bank of England, Bank of Italy and the Federal Reserve Bank of the Roumanian plan. I think they went a little further than was justified by the facts, but of course I have not questioned the statements and doubt if it is worthwhile to do so."[56]

So far as the Bank of England and the Reichsbank, as well as several other central banks, were concerned one of the principal reservations had to do with Rumanian prewar debts.[57] Rumania had not been servicing these debts adequately and the 1913 Rumanian Loan had been stricken from the official list of quotations of the London Stock Exchange. The Bank of England insisted that appropriate steps must be taken that would permit restoration of the issue to the Stock Exchange list before it could grant a credit to the Rumanian National Bank.[58] Similar prewar Rumanian bonds of various issues were outstanding in Germany, Switzerland, and Belgium, which occasioned similar reservations on the part of Hjalmar Schacht of the Reichsbank and Gottlieb Bachmann of the Swiss National Bank. Although there was no such debt question outstanding in Holland, Gerard Vissering of the Netherlands National Bank expressed doubts about his participation for the same reason. On the other hand, Louis Franck of the Belgian National Bank was willing

[55] Moreau, *Souvenirs*, p. 540.

[56] Letter, July 11, 1928, Strong to Harrison, Federal Reserve, Correspondence, Roumania, January 1928–.

[57] Germany also had some outstanding political differences with Rumania involving both German and Rumanian claims.

[58] Such steps were taken by early July 1928 (letter, July 11, 1928, Lubbock to Harrison, Federal Reserve, Correspondence, Roumania, January 1928–.

to participate in the credit despite the outstanding debt question in which Belgium was concerned. He did, however, express concern over the effect of such irresponsibility on Rumania's credit standing.[59] Rumania did resume payments on these outstanding debts before the central bank credit became effective, but in the spring of 1928 the issue was still very much in dispute.

There were other indications of the financial irresponsibility of the Rumanians and of the fact that the program was not as carefully worked out as it should have been. Moreau was approached by Kiriacescu on May 9, 1928, with a request for an advance of 80 million francs (about £650,000) to be used to support the leu, which was under some pressure as a consequence of a poor harvest. The advance was granted and the Bank of France offered to cede half of it to the Bank of England. The Bank of England accepted the offer on May 15.[60] A week later, Burilleanu approached the Bank of England for an advance of £1 million. Norman was, of course, confused since he was already sharing an advance with the Bank of France.[61] Moreau asked Kiriacescu to clear up the matter and it was finally settled by the Bank of France taking the full £650,000 of the original request and the Bank of England making an advance of £1 million. Both advances, particularly that of the Bank of England, were heavily drawn upon but were almost fully repaid by the end of September 1928. The repayment was only possible, however, because the Banca Commerciale of Milan (allegedly on the personal intervention of Mussolini) suddenly decided to advance $12 million to the Rumanian government and a large part of this advance was used to pay off the earlier ones.[62]

In July 1928 the Rumanian government negotiated for a $20-million advance from the bankers who were to handle the loan issue.[63]

[59] Letter, May 5, 1928, Schacht to Moreau; letter, June 27, 1928, Bachmann to Strong, *ibid.* Letter, July 11, 1928, Strong to Harrison; letter, July 20, 1928, Strong to Harrison, Strong Papers, European Trips, 1928. In the Swiss case, the problem was further complicated by the fact that agreements had been signed in 1924 and 1925, whereby the Rumanian Finance Department undertook to collect the amounts due from the debtors and the agreements were not being lived up to.

[60] Moreau, *Souvenirs*, p. 556.   [61] *Ibid.*, pp. 565–66.

[62] Letter, September 28, 1928, Rist to Harrison, Federal Reserve, Correspondence, Roumania, January 1928–.

[63] Letter, July 25, 1928, Rist to Harrison, *ibid.*

The credit was to be used to strengthen Rumania's exchange reserves. The advance was never formally requested or granted, however, since the exchange situation began to improve toward the end of the summer.[64] Nevertheless, for unspecified reasons but perhaps because of concern over these indications of financial difficulty, the three British banks (Barings, Schroder, and Rothschild) that had originally agreed to handle the British issue of the loan withdrew. Their place was taken by Lazard Brothers and Hambros, although there were indications that Hambros was less than fully satisfied with the stabilization program.[65] During the same month, Strong had a discussion with Rist and asked Rist where the money for the loan was coming from. He was told that most of it, possibly as much as $50 million, must come from America. Strong advised him that this was an unfortunate feature of the plan since conditions at the time made it quite uncertain whether successful flotation of a loan of this size was possible.[66] In November 1928, as the issue of the stabilization loan was imminent, Harrison complained to Rist that the Rumanian National Bank was negotiating with the American Exchange Irving Trust Company for a $6-million, three-month credit and that this might jeopardize the central bank scheme and the loan.[67]

None of these incidents, except the advances of the Bank of France and the Bank of England, was foreseeable in detail in the late spring of 1928; but taken in their entirety they indicate a state of affairs that should have been evident to anyone really familiar with the situation. Certainly, they indicate that there was indeed a need for stringent controls to be established to protect the stabilization program and the loan issue.

In any event, by the late spring of 1928 when Strong was departing for a summer in Europe, the situation had become so confused that his first order of business was to meet Norman in Cherbourg in an attempt to reach an understanding with the Bank of England.

[64] Letter, September 28, 1928, Rist to Harrison, *ibid.*

[65] Memorandum, July 18, 1928, Galantiere to Harrison, subject: "Roumanian Stabilization," *ibid.*

[66] Letter, July 27, 1928, Strong to Harrison, Strong Papers, European Trips, 1928. As finally issued, only $10 million of the loan was actually floated in the United States.

[67] Cable, November 21, 1928, Harrison to Rist, Harrison Collection, Binder 27.

The talks seem to have raised at least as many questions as they settled. In a typically British gesture, Norman sent Dr. Stewart to Cherbourg one day in advance ". . . so that our liaison officer might himself tell me directly the whole story in his own way, the bad as well as the good, and certainly Stewart did so." [68] One of the items discussed with Stewart was the rumor that Poincaré had written an official letter to the Rumanian government indicating the unwisdom of applying a League scheme. Strong stated that he did not believe that any such letter had been written, but ". . . even if it had been written, it would not have influenced our decision, because we felt that all the larger nations of Europe had political interests in other countries which they were seeking to protect or to promote. What we would have objected to was any effort on the part of the French Government to coerce or induce or influence the Bank of France to undertake a transaction with the Bank of Roumania with any political object in view." [69]

Again, there was considerable naïveté in this point of view. Strong obviously recognized that the central bank credits, whether extended or refused, would serve some nation's political interests. Yet he pretended that somehow these political considerations could be kept isolated from the decision-making process in the central banks involved. While it may have been difficult or even impossible for some governments to coerce their central banks in cases such as these, it was patently ridiculous to think that they made no effort to influence the bank's actions.

Stewart advised Strong that the origin of the rumor lay in the fact that when Siepmann was in Paris having a discussion with Quesnay, he had seen a letter on Quesnay's desk that he took to be a copy of a communication addressed by the French government to the Rumanian government making some reference to the Rumanian business. Norman and Stewart had since been advised that it was not a copy of a letter to the Rumanian government, but an interdepartmental communication providing the Bank of France with the official French attitude toward the Rumanian plan of stabilization.[70]

In a later conversation with Strong, Siepmann confirmed this

[68] Memorandum re: Bank of England–Bank of France Relations, May 24, 1928, Strong Papers, European Trips, 1928.
[69] Ibid.   [70] Ibid.

story and said that he had understood at the time from Quesnay that the letter was a copy of a letter written by Poincaré to the Rumanian government and had so stated in a memorandum that he had written that night. Siepmann told Strong that he had a good memory and was convinced at the time that his memorandum was correct, but that he was now satisfied that it had not been a copy of a letter to the Rumanian government and that no such letter had been written.[71] Strong also later put the matter bluntly to Moreau, Rist, and Quesnay, who advised that Strong's understanding was entirely correct. They indicated that the Bank of England had gone so far as to put the date of the letter at November 17, 1927 (which would fit well with the date of the entry in Moreau's diary). They insisted, however, that the document was simply an interdepartmental communication.[72] Under such circumstances, it is hardly surprising that Norman and Moreau did not trust each other.

Stewart questioned the position of the Federal Reserve in being willing to take a share in a credit without accepting such a responsibility as in the case of Belgium, Poland, and Italy as would justify American bankers' making a public issue of Rumanian government bonds. Strong's reply was:

. . . our position was that we had been approached by a close and important associate to take a participation in a small credit which would probably be nominal in amount; that in taking such a participation we were in no different position than Switzerland or the Netherlands or Sweden were in when Belgium and Poland stabilized, and while of course all sorts of interpretations might be put upon our participation in any business of this sort, it had been made perfectly clear to the Bank of France and the Bank of England before this discussion arose that we would not be original parties, we would not initiate or be responsible for a plan, we would simply give the plan such casual examination as would ordinarily be the case in participating in such a plan, and that position was justified by precedent in the other stabilization cases.[73]

That the Federal Reserve was in the same position as a small central bank participating in a central bank credit it was not sponsoring

[71] Letter, July 27, 1928, Strong to Harrison, *ibid.*
[72] Memorandum re: Bank of England–Bank of France Relations, May 24, 1928, *ibid.*
[73] *Ibid.*

was technically correct. But in the practical sense of market impact and influence on other central banks, the Federal Reserve, the Bank of England, and even the Bank of France simply could not place themselves in such an innocuous position. This should have been evident to Strong and Harrison when they found it necessary to take steps to deny rumors circulating in Bucharest that the Bank of France and the Federal Reserve Bank were undertaking a stabilization plan for Rumania.[74]

Stewart also advised Strong that the juniors in the Bank of England (especially Niemeyer and Siepmann) were actively conducting unofficial correspondence with a great many central banks containing important statements and representations which Stewart considered extremely dangerous. In addition, he said that the meeting to arrange a private banking transaction with the Yugoslavs had been conducted in the Bank of England and that Norman had put the handling of Yugoslav matters in the hands of a Mr. Bark, who was indirectly an employee of the Bank of England. Bark, while not employed directly by the Bank of England, was running a Vienna bank that the Bank of England had taken over during the war.[75]

There was also some discussion with Stewart, of course, concerning the relationship between the Federal Reserve and the Bank of England in the Rumanian matter, but this was preliminary to discussion with Norman. Strong did tell Stewart that the Federal Reserve ". . . had no intention of being an expert adviser to the Bank of England in stabilization plans in Europe, nor indeed would we permit ourselves to be understood as endorsing plans of the Bank of France, they being quite capable in these matters, just as much as we were." [76]

The discussions with Norman, however, were most unsatisfactory. Strong felt that Norman constantly fell back on assertions of lack of knowledge because he had been absent from the bank and eventually took recourse in reticence. By the end of the morning, Strong told him that ". . . it was impossible for us to deal with each other with any satisfaction when I was engaged in telling him everything

[74] *Ibid.*

[75] Memorandum re: Bank of England–Bank of France Relations, May 24, 1928, *ibid.* See p. 128.

[76] Memorandum re: Bank of England–Bank of France Relations, May 24, 1928, *ibid.*

in my mind and heart and when I could get nothing out of him except disclaimers of knowledge and the discussion of vague principles with which we either had no concern or had never heard of or did not believe in." [77] After lunch, Strong asked Norman to tell him frankly if he had any complaint in regard to the attitude of the Federal Reserve Bank. Norman replied ". . . that they had no complaint whatever, that we were certainly justified in joining with any bank of issue on any terms in any piece of business such as Roumania, and it was not their business to criticize. He said that he himself was committed to a League plan for Roumania and that was a matter of principle which applied to Roumania and other governments of like instability, uncertainty or unreliability. . . ." [78]

This was as far as the discussion got on fundamental issues. Norman admitted that Bark was indirectly an employee of the Bank of England since they had employed him to run a bank owned by the Bank of England. When asked about Niemeyer's activities, he told Strong that Niemeyer was acting as a member of the Finance Committee of the League of Nations. In exasperation, Strong asked how it was possible ". . . for me or for the French to distinguish between Niemeyer as League, Niemeyer as Bank, or Bark as private person and Bark as an employee of the Bank of England. I said that these methods were the very things which were causing trouble." [79] But on the vital issues they got no further than a commitment from Norman that he would do what he could.

Part of the difficulty may have been Strong's fault in that he had taken the position during the discussions that the Bank of England had been fully advised of the Reserve's position prior to Moreau's talk with Lubbock. This was not quite true and as soon as he was made aware of this, Strong wrote Norman a letter of apology:

He [Harrison] feels that both you and Stewart were surprised—and possibly more than surprised—that I had taken the position in our talks that you had been fully advised, in advance of Moreau's talk with Lubbock, as to our attitude in regard to initiative or leadership in the Roumanian matter.

I certainly must have made a mistake of memory or statement, and I want to correct it at once. My recollection of the sequence of events at Cherbourg was that immediately upon hearing from Moreau by mail that

77 *Ibid.*   78 *Ibid.*   79 *Ibid.*

they had been approached by the Bank of Roumania, Harrison wrote him a letter raising the question as to whether it was not a suitable case for the League to handle. The question of leadership or initiative by the Federal Reserve Bank was not, however, according to his or my memory, mentioned in that letter. On the other hand, I had clearly in mind that a copy of the letter had been sent to you immediately that it was despatched to Moreau. In that my memory or information may have been incorrect.

Also, the definite disclaimer of leadership was, I now realize, contained in the cable sent to you *subsequent* to Moreau's visit, a copy of which was also cabled to Moreau. . . .

I can only say in explanation that there was never a time, from the moment we first heard of this business, when we had any intention of undertaking the responsibility of initiation or of leadership, and I think our position on that point has been unvarying from the start. I was also convinced that you had been kept informed in more detail than was the case. Probably the sequence of events was not as clear in my own mind as it would have been had I been attending to these things personally and not been so ill.[80]

It must be remembered that this letter was written in Grasse, France, where Strong was vacationing, and it was here that Harrison and Strong met. They had to rely, therefore, on their memories of the sequence of events and the contents of various documents since the files of the Federal Reserve Bank of New York were not immediately available to them. The letter to Moreau, however, did not in fact mention the question of Federal Reserve leadership or initiative. Nor, indeed, do the files indicate that a copy of the letter was sent to the Bank of England. This is not particularly significant, however, since the letter did nothing to clarify the position of the Federal Reserve with respect to leadership. While it is undoubtedly true that Strong never had any intention of assuming leadership in the Rumanian affair, the fact remains that this intention was not made clear to the Bank of England until after the Moreau-Lubbock meeting.

Norman wrote a warm letter of acknowledgment and forgiveness in response to Strong's letter and the matter appeared to be settled. There was one point, however, which had still not been brought out to Strong, perhaps because Norman himself was unaware of it. In mid-June 1928 Strong met Lubbock in Grasse and discovered the origin of the concept of joint responsibility:

[80] Letter, June 6, 1928, Strong to Norman, Strong Papers, Bank of England.

Of course, the difficulty which arose at Cherbourg and which has now been fully explained and, I believe, fully cleared up, was partly due to my defective memory as to the sequence of events, but was also partly due to the fact that I was never aware, until Lubbock reached Grasse, that it was the French themselves who had proposed that we be brought in as leaders and consequently that the origination of the idea of dragging us in as a *sine qua non* to Bank of England participation was simply the outgrowth of a proposal by Moreau, rather than a happy thought on the part of the officers of the Bank of England. Norman's concern resulting from the Cherbourg talk arose entirely from the fact that my talks appeared to imply that the Bank of England had imposed conditions which they knew in advance could not be fulfilled by the French.

The whole affair was really a mess until Lubbock and I met, and I blame Norman very much for this and some of his associates equally, because of their failure to give us really full information as to just what was happening.[81]

The affair was indeed a mess and the Cherbourg meeting came very close to making it even more of a mess than it had been before. This was as close as the Federal Reserve Bank of New York and the Bank of England came to a loss of confidence in each other and a serious breach between these two would have had most dire consequences for central bank cooperation. The rupture was patched up, however, and the Federal Reserve was able to avoid a position of formal responsibility, which it did not want to take. Again, as in the Polish case, it was Norman who accepted a position he did not want in the interests of central bank cooperation. On July 11, 1928, Lubbock wrote to Strong: "We have received an invitation from the Bank of France to participate in a Central Bank credit for Roumania, and we have accepted it. (You have heard of Roumania, haven't you? It is a country in South Eastern Europe, in which a certain M. Moreau has been taking an interest.) But there are a good many things to be done yet, before the credit is fixed up." [82]

By the end of July 1928 an agreement had been concluded with the private bankers for a loan in the nominal amount of $80 million, of which $30 to $40 million was tentatively planned for flotation in the United States. One of the principal problems in arrang-

81 Strong's Memorandum re: My Conversations with Mr. Cecil Lubbock, Grasse, June 12, 1928, Strong Papers, European Trips, 1928.
82 Letter, July 11, 1928, Lubbock to Strong, Strong Papers, Bank of England.

ing the loan was to provide it with greater securities and guarantees than outstanding Rumanian bonds so that investors would be attracted to it. In particular, a 1922 bond issue was being quoted in London which was guaranteed by the whole of the state's assets and some means had to be found to provide the new loan with exceptional security without diminishing the guarantees for the 1922 issue. The solution arrived at was to organize a Rumanian Autonomous Fund which was granted the exclusive right to exploit the state monopolies consisting primarily of the tobacco and powder monopolies.[83] This Fund, rather than the Rumanian government per se, would issue the loan. Only the issue price remained to be agreed upon and it was expected that the loan could be issued in October.

Agreement on the central bank credit, while not legally concluded, had reached a point where Strong felt that a moral commitment existed which could no longer be avoided. This was of some concern to him since he felt that it put the Rumanian government in the position of having an option on the credit so that in dealing with the private bankers it could use the credit as a sort of moral security as to the soundness and saleability of the government loan. He was also concerned over the fact that none of the papers about the credit specified a time limit within which the public loan had to be issued, as had been done in previous cases. On the basis of the central banks then committed to the credit, it would be in the amount of $20 million; however, the Reichsbank and the Swiss National Bank had not yet joined, since the prewar debt problem was still unsettled. If they eventually joined, the amount would rise to $25 million. All in all, Strong was not very happy with the arrangements as they then existed. He wrote: "While I am satisfied that Dr. Rist has done the very best he could in this matter, I have a little feeling that his inexperience in the handling of practical questions has led him to be a little lenient in some details, such as the relation of the bankers' credit to the public loan, fixing the date, etc., and that the situation will need to be watched rather carefully." [84]

[83] Letter, July 25, 1928, Rist to Harrison, Federal Reserve, Correspondence, Roumania, January 1928–.
[84] Letter, July 27, 1928, Strong to Harrison, Strong Papers, European Trips, 1928.

It is particularly surprising to find Strong at this late date expressing concern over the relationship between the credit and the loan. He and Harrison had been insisting that the relationship was purely incidental and could not be a factor affecting the question of Federal Reserve participation in the credit. Now Strong was expressing concern over the possibility that the Rumanian government might use the credit as a selling point in its negotiations with the private bankers. That this is significantly different from the bankers using it as a selling point in the market is difficult to see.

In any case, the Rumanian debt problem with Germany and Switzerland was finally settled in the fall of 1928 and by November 14 both these central banks had joined the consortium.[85] Final agreement on the central bank credit in the amount of $25 million was reached on November 16, 1928.[86] The credit was not to become effective, however, until a number of conditions were met. The National Bank of Rumania was to establish its statutory power to guarantee bills discounted; the government was to provide written assurances that it would interpose no obstacle to repayment even if in gold; the stabilization program was to be legally promulgated; and the loan was to be issued.[87] The original agreement specified that these conditions must be met by December 15, 1928, but this date was later extended to March 15, 1929.[88]

[85] Cable, November 14, 1928, Rist to Harrison, Federal Reserve, Correspondence, Roumania, January 1928–.

[86] Agreement between the National Bank of Roumania, the Participants, and the Netherlands Bank, *ibid*. Participation was as follows:

United States	$4,500,000 in Dollars
Austria	500,000 in Schillings
Belgium	500,000 in Belgas
Czechoslovakia	1,000,000 in French francs
Finland	250,000 in Dollars
France	4,500,000 in French francs
Germany	4,500,000 in Reichsmarks
Great Britain	4,500,000 in Pounds Sterling
Hungary	500,000 in Pengos
Italy	2,000,000 in Lire
Netherlands	1,000,000 in Florins
Poland	500,000 in Zlotys
Sweden	250,000 in Dollars
Switzerland	500,000 in Dollars

[87] *Ibid*.

[88] Cable, December 17, 1928, Federal Reserve Bank of New York to Bank of France, *ibid*.

By this time, the stabilization program had, of course, also been finalized and accepted by the Bratianu government. At this moment, however, the Bratianu cabinet fell and Iuliu Maniu took over the government. He decided not to alter the monetary policies of his predecessor and to resume negotiations with the bankers. The negotiations resulted in some changes in the loan and, hence, some minor changes in the stabilization program. Parliament was dissolved and new elections called. The new Parliament was not to meet until mid-December so that any prospect for issue of the loan had to be pushed off to early 1929.[89]

Until this time, the plans still called for a United States bond flotation of $30 to $40 million. The New York bond market in the fall of 1928 was, however, very weak and, about the end of November, Chase Securities, Blair and Company, and Dillon, Read, the United States bankers, advised their European counterparts that a New York issue of this size was utterly impossible under prevailing conditions. As an example, they cited a recent $12-million Bulgarian issue for which one house had taken one hundred bonds and been able to sell only one.[90] As a sign of good faith, however, the United States bankers agreed to take $10 million.[91] For this and perhaps other reasons, the loan issue underwent considerable change before the final agreement was signed on February 1, 1929. The total amount of the loan was increased to $101 million, of which $30 million was purchased at par by the Swedish Match Company as partial payment for the exclusive right to operate the Rumanian match monopoly for a period of thirty years from July 1, 1929.[92] The total

---

[89] Cable, November 14, 1928, Rist to Harrison, *ibid.*
[90] Memorandum J. E. Crane to the file, December 1, 1928, *ibid.*
[91] Memorandum J. E. Crane to the file, December 3, 1928, *ibid.*
[92] Loan Prospectus, *ibid.* The remaining issue was as follows:

Great Britain	£2,000,000
France	Fr 561,638,000
Austria	$1,000,000
Belgium	$3,000,000
Czechoslovakia	$1,000,000
Germany	$5,000,000
Holland	$3,000,000
Italy	$8,000,000
Roumania	$2,000,000
Switzerland	$4,000,000
United States	$12,000,000 of which $2,000,000 was withdrawn for sale in Sweden.

yield of the loan to the Rumanians was about $90 million, which was considerably more than had been expected from the original plan.[93]

Legal stabilization was promulgated on February 7, 1929, on the basis of the final version of the stabilization program, which was dated February 1, 1929. This final version of the program provided for use of the loan proceeds as follows: [94]

1. Legal Stabilization of the Currency		$25 million
a. National Bank	$10 million	
b. Credit Institutions	$15 million	
2. Operating Fund		$20 million
a. Treasury	$11 million	
b. Railways	$9 million	
3. Railways and Other Constructive Public Works		$45 million
a. Capital expenditure and reconditioning of the railway system	$35 million	
b. Other public works	$10 million	

The sums allocated to credit institutions were to pay off their advances from the National Bank and those for the National Bank were to clear its portfolio of illiquid assets. Of the $11 million allocated to the Treasury, $6 million was to pay off advances that the Treasury had made to the Autonomous Fund and $5 million was to go to the Treasury's operating fund. The other items are self-explanatory. From this distribution, it can be seen that only one-quarter to one-third of the loan (depending on how one views Treasury operating funds) was devoted to strictly monetary purposes. At least half of the proceeds was used for developmental purposes. Thus, the accusation of the Bank of England that the stabilization program and the central bank credit were being used to make a development loan issue more palatable to the market was clearly justified.

The position of the Adviser under the plan was precisely that. He was without any authority even to control the use of the loan pro-

[93] Memorandum, L. Galantiere to Harrison, September 17, 1929, subject: "A Note on Rumania," *ibid*. Thirty per cent of the issue was at par, 20 per cent at 92 (Paris), and 55 per cent at 88.

[94] Programme of the Rumanian Government for Monetary Stabilization and Economic Development, *ibid*.

ceeds or the revenues pledged as security for the loan. He was appointed to the Board of Directors of the Rumanian National Bank for a period of three years but had no assigned functions with respect to the government. The pertinent paragraph that spells out his functions reads as follows:

He will collaborate closely with the Board of Directors and the Executive Committee at the National Bank, will have the right to be present at all meetings of the Board and of the Committee and will have an advisory vote on all questions relating to the application of the stabilization plan, the service of arrears, and the execution of transfers provided for in the loan contract. In the event that the foreign central banks, upon the request of the National Bank of Rumania, should decide to grant credits to the latter, the Technical Adviser could serve as intermediary between these banks and the National Bank for the operations involved in the extension of such credits.[95]

In other words, he was a pure figurehead whose function was to give the impression to the bond market that Rumanian finances were being supervised when, in fact, no effective supervision was provided at all.

It is difficult to assess the Rumanian program in operation because it was instituted at a time when the world was sliding into economic difficulties in which Rumania, of course, shared. There were problems both with the foreign trade balance and public finances. The trade deficit for 1928 was 5.226 billion lei and the budget deficit for that year, which had been estimated at 3.785 billion lei, was more nearly 5 billion.[96] The difficulties continued until, in early 1932, Charles Rist, the Technical Adviser, recommended to the new Rumanian government instituted after Carol's return that they go to the Financial Committee of the League to put their finances in order.[97] It is difficult to say, however, how much of the problem was the result of a weak stabilization plan and how much resulted from general world economic conditions.

[95] *Ibid.*

[96] Summary of the First Report of the Technical Adviser to the National Bank of Rumania, May 7, 1929, *ibid.*

[97] Auboin, *Les Missions,* p. 17. Rist was designated the Technical Adviser, but he only resided in Bucharest during the first year of the program. Auboin was named as Resident Adviser under the general supervision of Rist.

Nevertheless, it is clear that the program was weak. As in the Polish case, if control was necessary, it was the substance, not the shadow, which was needed. In the case of Rumania, only a very dim shadow was provided. I have made abundantly clear my own sympathy for Norman's view of the real purpose of the Rumanian loan and of the need for stringent controls. That his attitude was considerably influenced by a desire to thwart French political interests in Eastern Europe is almost certain. That it was influenced by his concern over growing French financial power is unquestionable. But this does not alter the fact that he saw the situation more realistically than any of the others. It does not alter the fact that he took his responsibilities with respect to the smaller central banks and the financial market very seriously, whereas the others set those responsibilities aside. It is understandable that the Bank of France was vitally concerned about keeping the Rumanians away from the League and, therefore, from the Bank of England; but it was not necessary to go to the extreme of permissiveness for this purpose. The Bank of France could have insisted upon a modicum of responsible conduct on the part of the Rumanians during the negotiations and upon meaningful controls, even though they might have been less severe than those of the League. Strong and the other Federal Reserve authorities, on the other hand, did not even have the excuse of political interest. They were willing to sacrifice the Reserve's responsibility to the other central banks and to the market to some vague notion of cooperation that had come to mean that one must not, under any circumstances, question the opinion of another major central bank.

Not that their refusal to accept responsibility for the decision of the Bank of England was unjustified. This was a perfectly reasonable position to take, as was Norman's position that he did not want to participate unless an institution in which he had confidence recommended the program. But neither the Bank of England nor the Federal Reserve could avoid the responsibility to the smaller central banks and to the market which their participation in the credit implied. They, therefore, had a duty to satisfy themselves that the program was sound. They could not do this simply by a study or the written program, which was of necessity a summary document. All the nuances of understanding which come from participation in the negotiations are missing from a document of this type. The alternative was to accept the judgment of an institution in which they had confidence and which conducted the negotiations. Had the Bank of France behaved responsibly in the matter, there is no reason (other than political) why its judgment should not have been accepted. But it became evident very early that the Bank of France was striving to accommodate the Rumanians rather than striving to arrive at a sound program. Norman saw this, but did not have the fortitude to refuse to participate on any basis whatsoever. He chose to try to hide behind the Federal Reserve. Strong had sufficient doubts to refuse to endorse the program, but he too did not have the fortitude to refuse to participate. Central bank cooperation had really taken on a strange meaning. In its name, they all joined in an effort in which they really had no confidence and, in the process, went a long way toward destroying any realistic basis for meaningful cooperation.

Chapter VI. CONCLUSION

Understandably enough, the Rumanian stabilization operation was the last such program in the 1920s in which a credit extension to the central bank of the stabilizing nation by a consortium of central banks was involved. At least some of the central banks must have felt that they had been exploited and misled during the negotiation of the Polish credit and even more so during the negotiation of the Rumanian one. The mistrust and ill will generated, especially between the Banks of England and France, by the pressure on sterling as a result of French stabilization techniques in 1927–1928 would alone have sufficed to make forthright cooperation between these two institutions most difficult. The difficulties and misunderstandings resulting from the Polish and Rumanian negotiations not only fanned this mistrust and ill will; they destroyed the unity of viewpoint and unquestioning mutual faith of the Bank of England and the Federal Reserve Bank of New York. The focal points around which such consortia could be organized had moved too far apart to leave much hope for cooperation of this type.

There were, of course, other reasons why Rumania was the last of the cooperative stabilization efforts. By the end of 1928, there were few unstablized national currencies remaining in Europe and the problem was soon to become one of maintaining the existing international monetary structure rather than one of bringing the few remaining outsiders into the framework. At least potentially, however, central bank cooperation had as large a role to play in the defense of the existing structure as it had in the geographical extension of that structure. Precious little was done in this respect until a few, desperate efforts were made in the summer of 1931. By this time, the situation was such that the measures taken were inadequate and too late. Earlier cooperative efforts might well have failed also in view of the scope of the problem, but the significant fact is that they were either not attempted or were attempted on too limited a scale.[1] It is conceivable, although admittedly doubtful, that an adequate effort made before pressures had built up to the level of the summer of 1931 might at least have mitigated the extent of the catastrophe.

When the German mark came under heavy pressure in the autumn of 1930, for example, the Bank for International Settlements provided limited support by intervening in the exchange market and by arranging a $125-million credit for the German government through the firm of Lee, Higginson and Company.[2] But the resources of the Bank for International Settlements were very limited[3] and the amount of the credit, given Germany's international monetary problems and her importance on the world scene, was scarcely sufficient to firmly restore confidence in the mark. No apparent effort was made to organize central bank support for the Reichsbank at this time.

In December of 1930, the British and French Treasuries, as well as the Banks of England and France, conferred on the problem of French demands against British gold and, while their views as to the causes and cures of the problem were predictably far apart, the French at least indicated a willingness to provide some support for sterling through the purchase of British securities.[4] For political reasons—one suspects primarily because of a reluctance to become indebted to an unfriendly French Treasury or Bank of France, which might use that indebtedness to restrict British freedom of action—the British refused the offer.

The chain of events brought about by the Credit-Anstalt difficulties in Austria in the spring of 1931 did result in some new cooperative efforts among the central banks, but on too limited a scale, and the principal burden fell on the bank least able to bear the strain—the Bank of England. By mid-May, the Bank for International

[1] Clarke, *Central Bank Cooperation: 1924–31*, pp. 185ff.
[2] E. L. Dulles, *The Bank for International Settlements at Work*, p. 113.
[3] Mrs. Dulles estimated that the BIS had less than 100 million Swiss francs at this time which could be utilized to strengthen the exchanges (*ibid.*, p. 112).
[4] Clay, *Lord Norman*, p. 370.

Settlements, in conjunction with eleven central banks, extended a
100-million-schilling (approximately $14 million) credit to the Aus-
trian National Bank for a period of three months.[5] By mid-June,
however, the credit was fully used, negotiations for a 100-million-
schilling loan to the Austrian government were snagged in politics,
and the Bank for International Settlements was attempting to arrange a new credit for the Austrian National Bank. Progress was
slow, however, and the Bank of England finally made an advance of
150 million schillings to the Austrian National Bank on its own on
June 17, 1931.[6]

By this time, the difficulty had already spread to Hungary and the
Bank for International Settlements had extended a $5-million ad-
vance to the National Bank of Hungary. It tried also to arrange an
additional $10 million in the form of a cooperative central bank
credit, but had to take $1 million of this amount itself when only $9
million was forthcoming from the central banks. Similarly, the Bank
for International Settlements could only arrange a second credit of
$10 million for the Hungarian National Bank by taking $3 million
of the total on its own account.[7]

The German situation had also become critical and here there
was little that the central bankers could do unless their efforts were
coupled with political corrections. In fact, Federal Reserve participation in the $100-million credit extended to the Reichsbank at the
end of June was contingent upon substantial participation by the
Bank of France in order not to remove pressure on the French to
deal with President Hoover's moratorium proposal.[8] From this
point onward, events moved with such momentum that it is very

[5] BIS cables of May 29 and 30, 1931, Harrison Collection, Binder 2. The BIS
provided a 40 million schilling advance and the central banks agreed to purchase or discount up to 60 million schillings of commercial bills.

[6] Cable, June 17, 1931, Harvey to Harrison, Harrison Collection, Binder 20.
The second central bank credit was never consummated.

[7] Harrison Collection, Binder 2. The Bank of France did not even participate
in this second credit since the BIS had refused its offer of $2 million if the
other participants (Federal Reserve, Bank of England, and BIS) reduced their
share to $2 million each. The original proposal was for a $15 million credit
to be taken $5 million each by the Federal Reserve and the Bank of France, a
nominal amount to be taken by the Bank of England for the sake of appear-
ances, and the balance to be taken by BIS.

[8] Harrison's memorandum to the Confidential Files, June 24, 1931, subject:
"Germany," Harrison Collection, Binder 59.

doubtful whether any feasible scale of central bank cooperation could have been effective in altering their course.

The reluctance of central bankers to cooperate in defense of the system in the fall and spring of 1930–1931 cannot, of course, be explained solely—nor, perhaps, even primarily—in terms of the legacy of the stabilization loan and credit negotiations. Certainly the divisions between France and England, France and Germany, and France and Austria were more deep-seated than the mere question of financial influence. In fact, it was the existence of these more fundamental international divisions that was one of the principal barriers to the use of the Financial Committee of the League as a focal point for coordinating international monetary cooperation. The other principal barrier was the fact that one of the major nations concerned, the United States, was not a member of the League of Nations. It is by no means clear, however, that these obstacles need have been fatal to such use of the Financial Committee, particularly if the principle of its use had been established at an early date before fundamental divisions had hardened.

One of the virtues of the fiction that central banks were "private" institutions independent of the government—which, in fact, most of them legally were in the 1920s—was that it allowed them greater flexibility than government institutions could enjoy. It has already been pointed out [9] that the action of the United States government in refusing to permit the Federal Reserve System to join the Bank for International Settlements in 1931 because the BIS was established primarily as an institution to deal with reparations payments was extralegal. The government had no authority under the law to withhold or to grant such permission and it is at least questionable if the attempt to control the System would have been made in the mid-1920s or, if made, that it would have succeeded in the face of likely opposition from Benjamin Strong. In any event, the fact that George Harrison and the other Reserve authorities accepted the dictum in 1931 did not prevent their wholehearted and open cooperation with the BIS from the beginning of its operations.[10] The point

[9] See fn. 14, p. 12.

[10] In part, this can be explained by the fact that Gates W. McGarrah, the first President of the Bank for International Settlements, had just resigned as Chairman of the Board of the Federal Reserve Bank of New York. But the fact that

is that the assumption of a role of leadership on the part of the Financial Committee of the League did not necessarily mean that central banks were supplying funds through the League, nor *a fortiori* that the Federal Reserve System was automatically excluded from participation as a result of the non-member status of the United States.

The divisions within the League, in particular the divergence in British and French views with regard to the attitude toward Germany that must be adopted if European peace were to be maintained, may have provided an even larger stumbling block to the use of the Financial Committee. Something like the Bank for International Settlements, had it been organized earlier—which is, of course, to use the benefits of hindsight to an heroic extent—would have been a far preferable focal point than the Financial Committee from this point of view. But nothing like the Bank for International Settlements existed and the attempt to organize central bank cooperation on an ad hoc basis without resort to the League hardly served to evade these larger issues. In fact, the attempt had served only to aggravate those divisions and to introduce some new ones as well. On the other hand, an early appeal to the fiction of the "private" nature of central banking institutions might well have permitted the use of League machinery and the Financial Committee as a focal point for central bank credit operations despite the political differences.

The League machinery had, in fact, been used prior to the operations discussed in this study, notably in the case of Austria and Hungary, to provide financial assistance to central banks in difficulty and was being used for the purpose at the same time that the operations discussed here were taking place.[11] But in none of these cases was an attempt made to combine private loans with central bank assistance. The record, then, suggests that the use of League machinery might have kept central banks out of stabilization developments except on a bilateral basis. It is by no means obvious, however, that this would

---

McGarrah accepted the presidency is, perhaps, an indication of the limited impact of the government's ban.

[11] League of Nations, *The League of Nations Reconstruction Schemes in the Inter-War Period.*

have been unfortunate since the League schemes were obviously effective. On the other hand, it would appear that cooperative central bank credit extensions could have been combined with these League schemes, if desired, and if the pattern had been established prior to the deterioration in central bank relations. For political reasons, France or the United States or other nations may have chosen not to participate, but in itself this need not have been a bar to the cooperation of others. The ill will was generated not by the process of putting together a consortium, but by the struggle for leadership in the consortium. It is for this reason that the need for finding an indisputable leader to serve as focal point was so important.

Even when the Janssen attempt was made in Belgium, it was evident that controls, at least controls as stringent as those of previous League schemes, were unnecessary. They were even less necessary for the Francqui effort. This need not, however, have been a bar to the use of the League machinery to assist Belgian stabilization. The Financial Committee could have adopted a policy of adjusting the degree of control to the needs of the situation subject, perhaps, to the requirement of being able to justify its action to the League Council. On the basis of the Austrian and Hungarian plans, a League scheme had come to mean rigid controls; but this need not have been the case.

It was apparently primarily this lack of need for financial controls in the Belgian case (plus, perhaps, the close ties between Britain and Belgium) that led Norman to accept without question the idea of providing official international assistance for Belgium outside the League. When he and Strong did so, however, they opened a Pandora's box. They urged participation upon others as an indication of belief in and support of some vague notion of central bank cooperation. But others could play that game as well and not always with the same sense of responsibility that Norman brought to the game. Not only did the procedure open up the possibility for one central bank to organize international effort in support of its own interests —an element that was probably already present in the British action with respect to Belgium—it provided an additional arena in which conflicting national interests could manifest themselves. In addition, it opened the way for the debtor nations to play one national interest against another so as to gain financial assistance on terms most advantageous to them and, in this way, to aggravate the divisions which were already serious enough.

The need for international control over Polish finances was generally conceded even by those most interested in making the controls as innocuous as possible. If for no other reason, some form of control was necessary to make an international bond issue marketable. The full amount of the Dillon, Read issue of 1925 could not be marketed and there was not enough change in the situation a year later to offer much prospect of floating a larger loan unless some additional security could be provided. International control in one form or another was needed to furnish this added element of security.

The precedent of the Belgian stabilization, however, offered the Poles the hope of keeping those controls much less severe than they would have been had Poland been forced to turn to the League. Strong, who shared the general American mistrust of the League of Nations, was initially quite willing to take up the Polish cause and "protect" the Poles from the political influences in the League. Probably, there was also an element of pride over placing the Federal Reserve in a position of primary leadership in the internationalist movement involved in his eagerness to take up Polish stabilization. Strong's action, however, opened the way for power politics to be played much more directly and openly than would have been possible through the League. This, plus a belated concern over becoming too flagrantly embroiled in European politics, seems to have led him to regret his involvement, but it was too late to escape. Nevertheless, he tried to limit Federal Reserve responsibility in the matter and seems to have created the opportunity for the very willing Bank of France to step in more or less behind the scenes.

The strangest case of the four was the Italian stabilization. It would lie essentially outside the rubric of this study were it not for the part it played as a precedent to which the French could appeal in the Rumanian case. The Italians obviously had no need for an international stabilization loan and, even if they had, it is not clear that the added security of international controls or a central bank credit would have contributed much to its marketability.[12] Nor was there any evident need for a central bank or a private credit. It appears that the practice of securing a central bank credit had become the fashion and the Italians sought such a credit simply as a matter of prestige. Even then, they sought initially a very limited credit from the Bank of England and the Federal Reserve Bank of New York somewhat à la British stabilization. It was with some reluctance that they bowed to Norman's insistence upon a more widely distributed credit. In itself, this supports the idea that the Italians viewed the credit as a prestige measure. The implication is that they sought to present the lira as being in the same class as the pound sterling.

As events developed, it is evident that Norman and Strong would have been well advised to accept the initial Italian proposal to limit the credit extension to the Bank of England and the Federal Reserve. This would have left the Bank of England in a much stronger bargaining position in the Rumanian negotiations. By this time, however, Norman had apparently become so wedded to the pattern of joint central bank credits coupled with private loans that he not only insisted upon using this opportunity to organize another central bank consortium, apparently he also convinced the Italians to accept a private banking credit which they neither needed nor wanted. The pattern was maintained essentially intact, but at the price of the loss of considerable freedom of action. Having asked the Bank of France, and others, to accept without question the judgment of the Bank of England and the Federal Reserve Bank of New York as to the soundness of the Italian program, it was difficult for the Bank of England to question the judgment of the Bank of France as to the soundness of the Rumanian one.

The Rumanians (as well as the Yugoslavs, whose stabilization falls outside the scope of this study) frankly shopped among the major central banks to find the least onerous terms for gaining financial assistance. Even the French conceded that the appearance of

[12] The difficulty with the 1925 Italian issue seems, in large part, to have been American suspicion of the Mussolini regime rather than purely financial considerations (see Shepherd, *The Monetary Experience of Belgium, 1914–1936*, p. 126.

international control had to be provided in a Rumanian stabilization program if a bond issue were to be made marketable. But the important international issue in Rumanian stabilization was whether or not British financial, if not political, power was to displace French influence in Rumania. It is not clear that such displacement of French influence was really the goal of the Bank of England; but had it succeeded in forcing Rumania to the League, this would have been a likely consequence. By playing upon French fears of such an outcome, the Rumanians succeeded in securing all that they desired without submitting to anything more than the symbol of control.

Had the practice of dealing with stabilization operations through the League never been abandoned, the power conflict between Britain and France would certainly not have been eliminated. But in the financial sphere, the conflict would have had to take place within the League rather than directly contributing to the divisions among the major national monetary institutions. The conflict would necessarily have been largely confined to policy issues rather than having become involved in the details of each transaction. The possibilities for the smaller nations to exploit the power conflicts would at least have been greatly constricted. The Financial Committee of the League was hardly an ideal institution for the undertaking of such operations, but until the creation of the Bank for International Settlements, it was the only international institution available for the task. The first mistake was to deal with any stabilization program involving international cooperative effort outside that institution.

There is, however, an even more fundamental prior question than that of how the organization of the loans and credits should have been handled. Were the loans and credits really required for stabilization purposes? The goal of the operations, particularly in so far as Norman and Strong were concerned, was to promote European currency stabilization. If the loans and credits were not necessary for this purpose, then the damage done by their negotiation was to that extent also unnecessary. Even if they were not required for monetary purposes, however, this does not necessarily mean that the loans at least were superfluous. Some part of them might well have been desirable, if not essential, for development purposes—in itself a worthwhile cause. In this capacity, however, it can well be questioned whether they were a proper field of interest for central banking institutions,[13] and, in any event, this was not the purpose for which the central bankers ostensibly lent their aid.

The fact that none of the central bank credits were actually drawn upon is, of course, no conclusive indication that they were not needed. At the very least, their extension provided psychological support for the currency to be stabilized. The lack of need to exercise the drawing rights under the credits might have been simply a reflection of the effectiveness of this support. Even in the Italian case, where there was no international loan involved so that the credit served no purpose as support for a bond issue, it certainly contributed something to the bolstering of internal and external confidence in the lira. It is extremely doubtful, however, whether such support for the lira was really required. Not only had the Italians stabilized *de facto* in advance of the credit extension, they had forced the exchange value of the lira to an artificially high level prior to doing so. It seems evident that the Mussolini government had the power and the will to force any necessary sacrifices on the Italian people to make *de jure* stabilization effective without external support. It is difficult to see how the absence of such support would have significantly increased the burden on the Italian people.

In the Belgian case, the credit served this same purpose and, in addition, served to support the international bond issue. There is considerable question, however, as to how necessary the bond issue was. The public floating debt, other than that in the hands of the Bank of Belgium, had been consolidated and public finances put in order by strictly internal measures prior to the loan issue. It is true that the loan issue served to eliminate the government floating debt held by the central bank and to strengthen the bank's reserve position. With the government budget balanced, however, and at the exchange rate chosen for stabilization, it does not appear that these

[13] One of the virtues of the post-World War II international financial system is that it segregated such development financing from purely monetary operations and, in the International Bank for Reconstruction and Development, provided an international institution to assist in directing the flow of development capital.

improvements were a necessary prerequisite for effective *de jure* stabilization. One has the impression, in fact, that the key to Belgian stabilization lay in the bringing of order to their public finances. Once this was done, external aid was not required. Until it was done, external aid would not have helped.

The Polish case is more difficult. The credit again served to mobilize confidence and to support the bond issue. Part of the proceeds of the issue was used for purposes of economic development, but about 60 per cent was used for monetary purposes. But again, there is considerable doubt as to whether or not this much, if any, was required for stabilization. The loan proceeds, as well as the writing up of existing assets of the Bank of Poland, raised its cover ratio in December 1927 to a level that certainly seems excessive in a reasonably sound situation. If the situation were not basically sound, no cover ratio would have been adequate to maintain stabilization. In addition, both Norman and Strong considered the post-stabilization gold purchases of the Bank of Poland to be excessive. At the very least, therefore, the loan issue appears to have been larger than necessary from a purely monetary point of view. While the evidence is even more debatable than in the Belgian case, one has the impression that stabilization at the rate of 9 zlotys to the United States dollar could probably have been maintained even without a foreign loan.

The Rumanian case is again somewhat simpler. The proportion of the loan proceeds (some 70 to 75 per cent) devoted to development purposes is a clear indication that this was the real purpose of the bond issue. Even the Rumanians—in fact, especially the Rumanians—viewed the stabilization aspects of the loan as secondary. While the loan and the credit certainly made stabilization somewhat easier than it otherwise would have been, it seems very doubtful that they were essential for this purpose.

Thus, while it is impossible to make any categoric statement on the subject, it is at least highly questionable whether any of the loans and credits studied were required to make stabilization effective. On the other hand, there can be no doubt that they made at least the initial stages of the stabilization effort easier than they otherwise would have been. The availability of the loan and credit proceeds surely had some impact upon the state of public confidence, internal and and external, in the currency. With the possible exception of the Rumanian case, however, my impression is that adequate confidence existed before consummation of the loan and credit arrangements. Still, this added fillip may have been necessary to give the stabilizing governments the courage to take the step at the moment that they did so. Certainly, the conditions attached to the loans, and especially to the credits, did provide a useful argument to support necessary, but unpopular, domestic measures. From the outset, at least some of the creditor central bankers made a conscious effort to use the credit conditions for this purpose.[14]

In the case of Poland, and even more so in the case of Rumania, the loans did provide development capital. Not only was a portion of the loan proceeds devoted to this purpose, the programs developed as a condition for the floating of the loans created situations that attracted additional investment capital. Both nations, being economically relatively underdeveloped, were in urgent need of such foreign investment capital and it is unlikely that an adequate flow would have developed without the financial improvement that the stabilization programs, despite their defects, brought. It is true that Rumania had previously impeded such capital inflows and the mere lifting of such restrictions would have sufficed to attract some foreign capital. Nevertheless, the stabilization program and loan certainly served to increase the volume of the flow. It can be questioned whether the loans, as development loans, were a proper subject of interest for the world's central banks; but whether or not part of the proceeds was used for developmental purposes, the loans and credits could still be used to help mobilize additional private investment capital. To serve this purpose, however, the mere granting of a loan or credit is not enough. The conditions attached to the assistance provided must be such as to have a favorable impact on market evaluation of the credit standing of the borrowing nation. The behavior of both Poland and Rumania suggests an inability, or at least an unwillingness, to recognize that, if the full potential of the loan and credit were to be realized, the loan at least would have to pass the test of the market place with flying colors.

Whether or not the loans and credits were required for stabiliza-

14 See p. 32.

tion purposes is, then, a question of degree and a definitive answer cannot be given. Even if it were clearly established that they were unnecessary for these purposes, a study of the history of these negotiations provides guidance relevant to modern international problems. There is still a need for official intervention to provide and encourage financial assistance, be it for monetary or developmental purposes, to various nations from time to time. The experience of 1926–1928 points up the importance of institutionalizing such assistance whether it be in the form of monetary credits, development loans, or other forms of foreign aid. So long as each such transaction is dealt with on an ad hoc basis, national interests become embroiled in the details of each arrangement. The debtors—or the welfare recipients in the case of some forms of foreign aid—can be expected to exploit and aggravate those differing national interests for their own advantage. The negotiation of each transaction then becomes an additional source of world conflict.

Institutionalizing such international assistance is, of course, no panacea. It will hardly serve to eliminate any of the national divisions arising from a myriad of other sources. But it can serve to mitigate the extent to which such divisions are deepened as a result of the very worthy operation of providing financial aid to nations in need of it. Ideally, such assistance should be provided from funds available to the international institution from national loans and grants not tied to specific transactions.[15] Such an organization does not eliminate conflicts of national interest, but the conflicts must be manifest within the institution and will largely be confined to a policy level rather than being interjected into the negotiation of each individual transaction. Specific loans and credits can be negotiated by international officials constrained by the policies established by the governing bodies of the institutions. National conflicts can be largely confined within those governing bodies and to the discussion of general policy. The international officials negotiating any specific transaction can be free to judge the situation on its merits and to act

15 Such a pool of funds was set up on a small scale by the Bank for International Settlements in the summer of 1931 and this is, of course, the basis of the operations of both the International Monetary Fund and the International Bank for Reconstruction and Development.

according to their own judgment, subject to the requirement of being able to justify their actions in terms of the established policies.

Such a system requires that individual nations delegate authority to an international agency to expend the funds which that nation has contributed. The individual nation has sacrificed the power to opt in or out of any particular transaction. In itself, this is a difficult concession for national governments to make. In addition, the funds available to the international institution are limited to the fixed total of national contributions, which total may be inadequate for the needs of the moment. Increasing the quotas is at best a slow and tedious process; at worst, it is impossible on such blank check terms. Thus, it may be necessary to deal with each transaction individually. Even then, it is preferable that the negotiations be carried on through an international institution as leader of a consortium rather than have one national agency or another assume the lead.[16] At the very least, such a procedure reduces the possibilities for the borrowing nation to play one creditor nation against another. The borrower is forced to negotiate with the international agency, which can be expected to be as impartial as any agency could be—if only because each international official has other officials of a variety of nationalities constantly looking over his shoulder. The creditor nations are left relatively free to opt in or out of any specific transaction without such action implying any direct affront to some other creditor nation.

The post-World War II international financial machinery was initially established very much along these lines and apparently with some suspicion that politics could not be kept out of international economics by the simple expedient of looking to "independent" central banks to take over economic responsibilities. Not only were all three of the Bretton Woods institutions—the International Monetary Fund, the International Bank for Reconstruction and Develop-

16 The 1931 central bank credits were largely channeled through the Bank for International Settlements, and the ease of their negotiation, despite the strained financial condition of many of the participants and the small and inadequate amounts involved, stands in striking contrast to the 1926–1928 negotiations. See the Harrison Collection, especially Binder 2.

ment, and the United Nations Relief and Rehabilitation Administration—established as governmental organizations, most of the world's central banks, with the notable exception of the Federal Reserve System, were nationalized. Whether or not this latter step was in all respects a desirable measure is obviously a question far beyond the scope of this work. Suffice it to say that, from the point of view of this study, the two steps taken together have forced governments to assume responsibility for the actions both of the international organizations and of their own central banks. The loss of flexibility involved in the virtual elimination of the separate channel of cooperation among "private" central banks as an alternative to government cooperation may have been a small price to pay for this improvement. Nevertheless, in the event that governments are unable to reconcile their differences in the governing bodies of the international institutions, it is more difficult than ever now to find a way around the impasse. The overall impact of the two steps, however, has been to make the post-World War II international financial structure much stronger than even use of the League could have made that of the interwar period.

In any event, the postwar international financial structure developed somewhat differently than had apparently been anticipated at Bretton Woods. It was expected that the International Monetary Fund, the International Bank for Reconstruction and Development, and the United Nations Relief and Rehabilitation Administration would provide the international framework for monetary reconstruction and the institutions through which both relief and reconstruction assistance and later development aid would be channeled. It was apparently expected that, while certain bilateral programs such as the operations of the Export-Import Bank of the United States would continue, their assistance would be in addition to, not a substitute for, operations through the international agencies.

It soon became apparent, however, that the assumptions upon which this institutional framework was constructed were unduly optimistic. The magnitude of the relief and reconstruction task had been grossly underestimated and no one anticipated the extent of the pressure for development assistance that would arise in the postwar years. In addition, the extent to which military objectives would shape the form of national foreign aid programs was largely unforeseen at the end of the war. As a result, the national foreign aid programs that grew up in the postwar years quickly dwarfed the operations of the International Bank for Reconstruction and Development and led to a proliferation of foreign assistance agencies, both national and international.

Given the size of the postwar reconstruction and rehabilitation task, some such breakdown in the international structure for providing capital assistance was inevitable. Particularly in the early postwar years, most of the funds needed to finance the reconstruction program had to come from the United States. There was, then, some finite limit to the volume of United States funds that could be disbursed through United Nations agencies and still have those agencies retain their international character. If the size of the program were to be at all commensurate with the need, a bilateral United States program was essential. But, by the early 1950s, the United States developed a preference for bilateral, rather than multilateral, programs and, as other nations entered the foreign aid field, their preference also—notably in the case of France and, of course, Russia —was in the direction of bilateral programs.

In the field of foreign assistance, however, these national programs were, in general, frankly bilateral so that there was no need to strive ad hoc to arrive at some sort of coordinated multilateralism. This may have avoided some of the worst consequences of competition among the lenders and shopping on the part of the borrowers in the fashion of the Polish and Rumanian stabilization negotiations in 1927–1928. Nevertheless, the elements of competition and shopping were far from absent. In the field of technical assistance, for example, not only were there numerous national programs for the recipients to choose from, but the Technical Assistance Program within the United Nations specialized agencies was only loosely coordinated. With such a multitude of programs to choose from, the situation quickly developed where ". . . the desire to obtain the best possible bargain in an atmosphere of competition among the specialized agencies and between the United Nations and bilateral programs, resulted in the same or similar requests for assistance being made of different United Nations programs and of multilateral and bilateral programs alike." [17]

Similarly, in the field of capital assistance, Benjamin Higgins points out that "although spokesmen for the governments of some underdeveloped countries express their preference for a multilateral approach, there is some evidence that high officials of those governments directly concerned with administering and financing development programs are less concerned with where they get their funds than they are with how much they can get. The fewer strings attached the better; but so far, the strings attached by the World Bank have not appeared to be clearly less obnoxious to the responsible officials of all underdeveloped countries than the strings of the Export-Import Bank." [18]

There were other reasons why the underdeveloped countries might be expected to show a preference for bilateral rather than multilateral aid, and at least one of them might reasonably be expected to push the developed nations away from bilateralism. As early as 1957, Robert Asher pointed out:

Recent changes in the international situation, specifically the emergence of the Soviet Union as a potential supplier of aid to underdeveloped countries, could conceivably bring about an ironic shift in present positions. Underdeveloped countries that have hitherto been strong advocates of internationally administered grant aid may conclude that they can do better by jockeying individual foreign governments into outbidding each other in offering aid; developed countries, such as the United States, may be transformed into warm supporters of an internationally administered fund in order to avoid being whipsawed into an intolerable competition for the privilege of financing foreign development projects.[19]

At least partly in response to some such shift, the International Development Association was established in September 1960 as a

[17] Robert E. Asher, "Problems of the Underdeveloped Countries" in Robert E. Asher, Walter M. Kotschnig, William Adams Brown, Jr., and Associates, *The United Nations and Economic and Social Co-operation* (Washington, 1957), p. 453.

[18] Benjamin Higgins, *United Nations and U.S. Foreign Economic Policy* (Homewood, Ill., 1962), p. 164.

[19] Asher, "Problems of the Underdeveloped Countries" in Asher et al., *The United Nations and Economic and Social Co-operation*, p. 490.

subsidiary of the International Bank for Reconstruction and Development to provide an international agency that could disburse development capital on easier terms than could the IBRD itself. But, while IDA might provide a welcome alternative to other forms of multilateral aid for the underdeveloped countries, the experience of the last few years suggests that the developed nations see matters somewhat differently. There was much reluctance on the part of the creditor nations, especially the United States, to create such an agency as the International Development Association in the first place.[20] James Weaver points out that during the discussions in 1962 over the provision of replenishment funds for IDA "one factor that entered into determining how large the United States contribution should be was fear on the part of the State Department that a large contribution to IDA would hurt the bilateral aid program. Just as IDA fails to meet the political objectives of French foreign aid—it also fails to meet the political objectives of United States foreign aid." [21]

The steadily increasing difficulties which United States bilateral programs have faced in the Congress throughout the 1960s, coupled with the difficulties experienced in raising another fresh replenishment funding for IDA in 1968,[22] suggest, however, that other factors may have been involved in 1962. The creditor nations, and the United States in particular, may indeed have become disillusioned with being involved in competition for the privilege of furnishing bilateral aid, but there are few signs of wholehearted eagerness to take up the cause of multilateralism.

There are many excellent reasons that can be advanced in favor of internationalizing foreign aid to the maximum possible extent,[23] not the least of which is that such a step would reduce the extent to which international conflicts among the world's major nations can be aggravated by a competitive struggle which pits one against the other for the privilege of assisting less-developed nations. What ap-

[20] Peter B. Kenen, *Giant Among Nations* (Chicago, 1963), pp. 200–204.

[21] James H. Weaver, *The International Development Association* (New York, 1965), p. 195.

[22] *The Economist*, January 4, 1969, p. 50.

[23] See, for example, Kenen, *Giant Among Nations*, pp. 197–200, and Higgins, *United Nations and U.S. Foreign Economic Policy*, pp. 178–82.

pears to have happened in this case is that, not only was there undue competition among bilateral programs, but the international agency itself became a contestant in the struggle. The charter of the IBRD, which was wisely drawn up so as to protect the capital of the institution, made it impossible for the World Bank to match the conditions under which bilateral aid was being offered. By the time the International Development Association was formed so as to permit the IBRD to ease its lending terms, the creditor nations had become disillusioned, not only with bilateral aid, but with most development aid however furnished.

Had the initial efforts to supplement IBRD assistance been channeled through that institution, much of the opportunity for playing one creditor against another might have been avoided.[24] The immediate post-World War II resort to bilateral programs in the provision of reconstruction capital resulted in large part from the combination of the magnitude of the task and the concentration of possible material aid in the hands of one nation—the United States. A bilateral United States program, then, became inevitable. Had the United States channeled all its aid through international agencies, the effect would have been to convert the international programs into American ones. But the process went on far longer and on a far larger scale than necessary. The problem was not a unilateral one for the United States precisely because its share in total foreign aid loomed so large. Certainly, by the mid-1950s it could have channeled a larger portion of its effort through international agencies even if others did not do so. But there was a limit to the process unless other nations not only increased their foreign aid commitments, but channeled that aid through the United Nations and its specialized agencies.

The magnitude and urgency of postwar reconstruction is also a large part, but by no means all, of the explanation for the inactivity of the International Monetary Fund in the early postwar years. Attention was necessarily focused on the reconstruction task, a task that fell outside the concerns of the International Monetary Fund.

24 Only the competition among Western nations could possibly have been alleviated in this fashion. The East-West power conflict was, of course, too deep-seated to have been affected by simple changes in institutional structure.

In general, in the postwar years, balance of payments deficits were covered by currency depreciation rather than by resort to borrowings from the Fund.

I have argued [25] that, given the conditions existing in a continent just emerging from an extremely destructive war, this is the only intelligent course to follow. A premature attempt to stabilize the currency is either doomed to failure, or the parity that can be sustained will be inappropriate for later, more normal, conditions. The experience with the Anglo-American Financial Agreement of 1945—itself a bilateral, rather than a multilateral, arrangement—was a graphic demonstration of the danger in attempting stabilization too early after a major war.[26] Thus, the early inactivity of the International Monetary Fund, although hardly a consequence of the conscious recognition of this danger, may have been the course of wisdom. But it did encourage, to some extent at least, dealing with monetary problems outside of the Fund. Even after the Fund began to step up its activities in the mid-1950s, the practice of dealing with some international monetary problems outside of the Fund framework and on an ad hoc basis continued.

Given the limitations on the resources and powers of the Fund and the inevitable difficulties and delays involved in making changes in those powers and resources, it is, perhaps, impossible to avoid dealing with some problems outside of the formal Fund framework. But the Fund can be used as a focal point for negotiating such extra-institutional arrangements, the programs involved can be coordinated with the Fund's activities, and the resources provided can be channeled through the Fund. If this is not done, the way is opened for ad hoc groupings without clearly recognized leadership defined in advance and therefore for a gradual regression to the type of operation that was studied here.

Thus, when formal limitations on the Fund's capability to make loans to any given nation threatened in 1961 to leave unsupported a currency that was one of the keys to the entire international financial structure, some alternative had to be found. As time was not available to negotiate a change in the Fund's charter (assuming that

25 See fn. 9, p. 7.
26 Richard N. Gardner, *Sterling-Dollar Diplomacy* (Oxford, 1956), pp. 346–47.

this might have been successfully accomplished), the world's major creditor nations—the so-called Group of Ten—drew up the General Arrangements to Borrow. By this agreement, the group appeared to have formed a more or less permanent consortium for the purpose of providing supplementary assistance which would be furnished through the International Monetary Fund. But the participants reserved the right to opt out of any specific transaction so that the appearance that a permanent consortium had been formed was misleading.[27] Not only was the possibility of an alternative focal point to the IMF for international financial negotiation opened up, but the necessity for negotiating each supplemental transaction separately and in full detail was created. In such negotiation, there was no longer clearly defined and previously established leadership so that all the possibilities for competition for leadership to aggravate already existing international differences were opened up.

The assistance provided to sterling in 1961 and again in 1964–1965 was, as a matter of fact, furnished through the IMF so that the potential for mischief created by the General Arrangements to Borrow was not immediately evident. The support provided for the pound sterling in June 1966, however, was not furnished through the Fund; rather it was channeled through the Bank for International Settlements.[28] Worse yet, two of the nations aiding the pound at this time—France and the United States—did so independently of both the International Monetary Fund and the consortium. In the case of the United States, this independence of action was a consequence of an exceptional eagerness to assist the pound; in the case of France, it was clearly an indication of disapproval.

The support operations organized at the time of sterling devaluation in November 1967 brought this French disapproval to the foreground. She refused to join in the $1.6-billion central bank credit extended to the Bank of England at least in part because ". . . the French have been saying that the loan to Britain should be channeled through the I.M.F., thus permitting a measure of international control that would not be possible if the creditors were individual countries." [29] Her refusal was ". . . made so emphatically clear to

---

[27] Supplement to the *International Financial News Survey*, January, 12, 1962.
[28] *The Economist*, June 18, 1966, p. 1326.
[29] *The New York Times*, November 20, 1967, pp. 1 and 74.

the British that the Bank of England refrained from asking the French bank's cooperation." [30] She did join in the $1.4-billion International Monetary Fund loan which brought Britain to the limit of its drawing capacity in the Fund, but she did so in such a spirit that Britain was reportedly irked by her lateness and apparent reluctance to join.[31] As a final indication of disapproval, official diplomatic sources reported that France was the only major nation that refused to give firm prior assurance that she did not intend to devalue her currency.[32]

Difficult as the negotiations of the 1967 support for sterling were, they proceeded smoothly in comparison with the confusion, ill will, and recriminations that came out of the November 1968 meetings in Bonn, Germany, called to deal with the huge capital flows from France to West Germany. From the point of view of this study, perhaps the most upsetting aspect of this transaction was that it was handled by the Group of Ten almost to the exclusion of the International Monetary Fund as a voting, let alone a directing, institution.[33]

There are other indications, outside the framework of this study, of a tendency for international financial activity to revert to the practices of the 1920s. Earlier French demands on United States gold stocks, for example, bore a striking resemblance to the selling pressure on sterling in the late 1920s. This time, the franc itself came under pressure early enough to bring at least a temporary halt to the pressure on the dollar. French attempts to enlist the aid of the International Monetary Fund in the efforts to enforce stringent controls as a condition for support of a devalued sterling in 1967 were, perhaps, a belated recognition of the fact that the economic fate of all is tied to the avoidance of a disastrous crumbling of the basic international monetary machinery. The wrecking of that machinery by sterling suspension of gold payments in 1931 was surely not the only cause of the Great Depression, but neither was it a minor element in bringing on that catastrophe. Certainly,

[30] *The New York Times,* November 21, 1967, p. 76.
[31] *The New York Times,* November 20, 1967, p. 75.
[32] *The New York Times,* November 25, 1967, p. 57.
[33] "Communiqué of Ministerial Meeting of Group of Ten," *International Financial News Survey,* November 29, 1968, p. 397.

viewed in the light of what followed, the experience of the 1920s is not one to be eagerly emulated. One small step toward avoiding a repetition of those mistakes of the past is to move in the direction of more, not less, institutionalization and to do so before, not after, events have forced an unpremeditated change.

BIBLIOGRAPHY

BOOKS

Angelesco, Nicolas. *L'Expérience monétaire Roumaine (1914–1927)*. Paris: Jouve & Cie., 1928.

Asher, Robert E., Walter M. Kotschnig, William Adams Brown, Jr., and Associates. *The United Nations and Economic and Social Co-operation*. Washington: The Brookings Institution, 1957.

Barger, Harold. *The Management of Money: A Survey of American Experience*. Chicago: Rand McNally & Co., 1964.

Baudhuin, Fernand. *Histoire économique de la Belgique 1914–1939*. Vol. I. Bruxelles: Etablissements Emile Bruylant, 1944.

Blumenstrauch, Bernard. *Le Nouveau régime monétaire en Pologne et son rôle dans l'économie nationale*. Nancy: Société d'Impressions Typographiques, 1932.

Brown, William Adams, Jr. *The International Gold Standard Reinterpreted 1914–1934*. New York: National Bureau of Economic Research, Inc., 1940.

Burgess, W. Randolph. *The Reserve Banks and the Money Market*. New York and London: Harper & Brothers, 1946.

Cats, Hugo. *Les Effets du nouveau régime monétaire en Belgique sur son économie, depuis la stabilisation jusqu'a la crise économique*. Anvers: Imprimerie "Alpha," 1933.

Chandler, Lester V. *Benjamin Strong, Central Banker*. Washington: The Brookings Institution, 1958.

Chlepner, B. S. *Cent ans d'histoire sociale en Belgique*. Bruxelles: Université Libre de Bruxelles, 1956.

Clarke, Stephen V. O. *Central Bank Cooperation: 1924–31*. New York: Federal Reserve Bank of New York, 1967.

Clay, Sir Henry. *Lord Norman*. London: Macmillan & Co., Ltd., 1957.

Clough, Shephard B. *The Economic History of Modern Italy*. New York and London: Columbia University Press, 1964.

Crane, John O. *The Little Entente*. New York. The Macmillan Co., 1931.

Dulles, Eleanor Lansing. *The Bank for International Settlements at Work*. New York: The Macmillan Co., 1932.

Dulles, John Foster. *Poland: Plan of Financial Stabilization, 1927*. New York: Messrs. Sullivan & Cromwell, 1928.

Einzig, Paul. *Montagu Norman: A Study in Financial Statesmanship*. London: Kegan Paul, Trench, Trubner & Co., Ltd., 1932.

Friedman, Milton, and Anna Jacobson Schwartz. *A Monetary History of the United States 1867–1960*. Princeton: Princeton University Press, 1963.

Gardner, Richard N. *Sterling-Dollar Diplomacy*. Oxford: Clarendon Press, 1956.

Hargrave, John. *Montagu Norman*. New York: The Greystone Press, 1942.

Heilperin, Michel Angelo. *Le Problème monétaire d'après-guerre et sa solution en Pologne, en Autriche et en Tchécoslovaquie*. Paris: Recueil Sirey, 1931.

Higgins, Benjamin. *United Nations and U.S. Foreign Economic Policy*. Homewood, Ill.: Richard D. Irwin, Inc., 1962.

Kenen, Peter B. *Giant Among Nations: Problems in United States Foreign Economic Policy*. Chicago: Rand McNally & Co., 1963.

Kisch, Sir Cecil H., and W. A. Elkin. *Central Banks*. London: Macmillan and Co., Ltd., 1932.

League of Nations. Economic and Finance Section. *Brussels Financial Conference 1920: The Recommendations and their Application*. Vol. I. Geneva: League of Nations, 1922.

—— Economic, Financial and Transit Department. *The Course and Control of Inflation: A Review of Monetary Experience in Europe after World War I*. Geneva: League of Nations, 1946.

—— Economic, Financial and Transit Department. *The League of Nations Reconstruction Schemes in the Inter-War Period*. Geneva: League of Nations, 1945.

—— *International Currency Experience*. Geneva: League of Nations, 1944.

Longeaux, J. de. *Conséquences économique de la stabilisation Belge*. Paris: E. De Boccard, 1928.

Madden, John T., and Marcus Nadler. *The International Money Markets*. New York: Prentice-Hall, Inc., 1935.

Mills, J. Saxon. *The Genoa Conference*. New York: E. P. Dutton & Co., undated.

Mincer, Thadée. *Le Zloty Polonais: La Réforme monétaire en Pologne et ses suites*. Paris: Imprimerie "Labor," undated.

Mlynarski, Feliks. *Credit and Peace: A Way out of the Crisis*. London: George Allen & Unwin Ltd., 1933.

—— *The Functioning of the Gold Standard*. Geneva: League of Nations, 1931.

Moreau, Émile. *Souvenirs d'un gouverneur de la Banque de France: histoire de la stabilisation du Franc.* Paris: Librairie de Médicis, Editions M. -Th. Génin, 1954.

Myers, Margaret G. *Paris as a Financial Centre.* New York: Columbia University Press, 1936.

Perroux, François. *Contribution à l'étude de l'économie et des finances publiques de l'Italie depuis la guerre.* Paris: Marcel Giard, 1929.

Rist, Charles. *The Triumph of Gold.* New York: Wisdom Library, 1961.

Robin, Pierre. *La Réforme monétaire en Pologne.* Paris: Marcel Giard, 1932.

Ruell, Jacques. *The Age of Inflation.* Chicago: Gateway Editions, Henry Regnery Company, 1964.

Seton-Watson, Hugh. *Eastern Europe between the Wars 1918–1941.* Hamden, Conn.: Archon Books, 1962.

Shepherd, Henry L. *The Monetary Experience of Belgium, 1914–1936.* Princeton: Princeton University Press, 1936.

Volpi, Count Guiseppe, and Prof. Bonaldo Stringher. *The Financial Reconstruction of Italy.* New York: Italian Historical Society, 1927.

Weaver, James H. *The International Development Association: A New Approach to Foreign Aid.* New York: Frederick A. Praeger, 1965.

Wheeler-Bennett, John W. *The Wreck of Reparations: Being the Political Background of the Lausanne Agreement 1932.* New York: William Morrow & Co., 1933.

Wheeler-Bennett, John W., and Hugh Latimer. *Information on the Reparation Settlement.* London: George Allen & Unwin, Ltd., 1930.

Wolfers, Arnold. *Britain and France between Two Wars.* New York: Harcourt, Brace & Co., 1940.

PUBLIC DOCUMENTS

International Bank for Reconstruction and Development. *Policies and Operations of the World Bank, IFC and IDA.* April 1962, amended to June 30, 1963. Washington: International Bank for Reconstruction and Development, undated.

League of Nations. *Report of the Gold Delegation of the Financial Committee.* Geneva: League of Nations, 1932.

——— *Statistical Yearbook of the League of Nations 1930/31.* Geneva: League of Nations, 1931.

——— *Statistical Yearbook of the League of Nations 1935/36.* Geneva: League of Nations, 1936.

Republic of Poland. *Reports submitted by the Commission of the American Financial Experts headed by Dr. E. W. Kemmerer.* Warsaw: The Ministry of Finance, 1926.

United States. Agency for International Development. *Principles of Foreign Economic Assistance.* Washington: Superintendent of Documents, 1963.

———— *Combined Annual Reports of the World War Foreign Debt Commission: Fiscal Years 1922, 1923, 1924, 1925, and 1926.*

PERIODICALS AND PAMPHLETS

Auboin, Roger. *Les Missions de Charles Rist en Roumanie 1929–1932.* Paris: Librairie Sirey, undated.

Bopp, Karl R. "Hjalmar Schacht: Central Banker," *The University of Missouri Studies,* XIV, No. 1 (January 1, 1939), 1–91.

The Economist. 1966–1969.

Federal Reserve Bulletin. Vols. 6–17. Washington: Federal Reserve Board, 1920–1931.

International Financial News Survey. April 10, 1959; November 29, 1968; and Supplement, January 12, 1962. Washington: International Monetary Fund.

Krason, William S. *Banking, Monetary, Financial, and Economic Conditions in Poland after World War I.* United States Department of State, Foreign Service Institute Monograph Series, June 1951.

Kwiatkowski, Eugenjusz. *The Economic Progress of Poland.* Warsaw: The Polish Economist, 1928.

The New York Times. 1966–1968.

Volpi, Count Guiseppe. *Financial Statement made in the Chamber of Deputies by the Minister of Finance, Count Guiseppe Volpi of Misurata, June 2nd, 1927.* Rome: Provveditorato Generale dello Stato Libreria, 1927.

UNPUBLISHED MATERIAL

Federal Reserve Bank of New York. Selected Correspondence Files.

George Leslie Harrison Collection. Special Collections, Butler Library, Columbia University.

Benjamin Strong Papers. Federal Reserve Bank of New York.

INDEX

Advisor: to Poland (*see also* Dewey, Charles), 77, 82–83, 82*n*, 90–91; to Rumania (*see also* Rist, Charles), 104–105, 134–35, 135*n*
Albania, 51
American Exchange Irving Trust Company, 124
Anglo-American Financial Agreement, 157
Antonescu, General Ion, 104
Auboin, Roger, 135*n*
Austria, 59, 61, 97, 103, 139–41; League Reconstruction Scheme, 2–3, 15, 68, 72, 83, 92, 142–43; participation in loan issues, 133*n*; post-World War I inflation, 58
Austria, National Bank of, 30, 140, 140*n*; participation in central bank credits, 34*n*, 53*n*, 87*n*, 132*n*
Avenol, Joseph, 75–76
Averescu, Marshal Alexander, 101

Bachmann, Gottlieb, 6*n*, 122
Banca Commerciale Italiana, 62, 123
Bank for International Settlements: as alternative to the Financial Committee of the League, 4*n*, 141–42, 146, 151*n*; Federal Reserve membership, 4*n*, 12, 12*n*, 141–42, 141*n*; and interwar financial assistance, 139–40, 139*n*, 140*n*, 150*n*, 151*n*; and post-World War II financial assistance, 2*n*, 158
Bank of England (*see also* United Kingdom; Norman, Montagu), 3, 6*n*, 63, 103*n*, 108–109, 117*n*, 125–26, 127–28, 130, 138, 139; and Belgian stabilization, 22, 23, 25, 28, 30, 32–34,

37, 39*n*, 40–41, 98; and central bank leadership, 14, 40–41, 42, 55–56, 78, 80, 83–84, 98, 111–14, 116–18, 136; credits extended to, 2*n*, 32, 158–59; and development purposes of Rumanian loan, 104*n*, 106, 110, 134; and Italian stabilization, 42, 47–48, 50–53, 55–56, 98, 107, 117*n*, 145; on relation between private loans and central bank credits, 40, 110, 111, 117–18, 121, 121*n*; participation in central bank credits, 23, 34*n*, 53*n*, 87*n*, 132*n*, 140*n*; participation in other credits, 22, 123, 140; and Polish stabilization, 68–70, 73–76, 78, 79–80, 83–84, 86–87, 86*n*, 98–99, 106; and Rumanian stabilization, 104–107, 104*n*, 108–13, 109*n*, 114–18, 117*n*, 122–23, 124, 130, 132, 136–37, 146
Bank of Issue (*see* Central Banks)
Bank of Naples, 43–44
Bank of Sicily, 43–44
Bankers, private, 3, 13–14; and Belgian stabilization, 20, 20*n*, 21–24, 22*n*, 26, 28–29, 30, 33–34, 39–40, 147; credit extensions by, 22, 23, 26, 44*n*, 53, 88, 123–24; and development purposes of loans, 13, 76, 83, 104*n*, 110–11, 134, 146–47, 147*n*, 148, 149; foreign loan issues, 23*n*, 33*n*, 40*n*, 43–44, 62, 63, 64, 89–90, 90*n*, 95, 124, 124*n*, 130–31, 133–34, 133*n*, 134*n*; and Italian stabilization, 51, 52–53, 145, 145*n*; need for stabilization loans, 3–4, 39, 145, 146–49; and Polish stabilization, 61–62, 63, 64, 67–68, 75–77, 79, 81–83, 87–92, 95,